To all my wonderful friends

Whatever Next?

Also by Anne Glenconner

Whatever Next?

Lessons from
an Unexpected Life

ANNE GLENCONNER

HODDER &
STOUGHTON

First published in Great Britain in 2022 by Hodder & Stoughton
An Hachette UK company

This paperback edition published in 2023

1

Copyright © East End Farm Associates Ltd 2023

The right of Anne Glenconner to be identified as the
Author of the Work has been asserted by her in accordance
with the Copyright, Designs and Patents Act 1988.

A CIP catalogue record for this title is available from the British Library

Paperback ISBN 978 1 529 39735 2
eBook ISBN 978 1 529 39577 8

Typeset in Celeste by Palimpsest Book Production Ltd, Falkirk, Stirlingshire

Printed and bound in Great Britain by Clays Ltd, Elcograf S.p.A.

Hodder & Stoughton policy is to use papers that are natural, renewable
and recyclable products and made from wood grown in sustainable forests.
The logging and manufacturing processes are expected to conform
to the environmental regulations of the country of origin.

Hodder & Stoughton Ltd
Carmelite House
50 Victoria Embankment
London EC4Y 0DZ

www.hodder.co.uk

CONTENTS

INTRODUCTION

JUST WHEN I'D imagined life's great adventures to be over, I had the unexpected joy of becoming an author in my eighties, writing my autobiography, *Lady in Waiting*. Since then, I have made many personal appearances telling my stories and answering questions, which have also been great fun. Audiences have always been fascinated by my tales of Princess Margaret and my husband Colin Tennant, Lord Glenconner, but to my surprise, they've also been very curious about me and about my own background. They've wanted to know more about who I am as a person, as the modern expression goes, and what got me through the darker times of my life. Many of them have said they felt inspired by my gung-ho attitude, my sense of humour, and the energy with which I am still attacking life. I am particularly delighted to learn I have become an unofficial agony aunt as well as a gay icon.

This flattering reaction has given me pause and made me look again at the events that have shaped me, what I was taught about life in my youth, and what in turn life has taught me. This book is the result. Writing it has given me a chance to reflect on the world in which I was brought up and how I have ended up who and where I am. It has also given me the chance to talk openly about some things I have kept private until now.

As readers of my autobiography will know, I was born into the Coke family of Holkham Hall, a glorious estate in Norfolk, in July 1932. At the time my great-grandfather was the Earl of Leicester, and my father inherited the title in 1949. As a girl, even though I was his eldest child, I would not be able to inherit it. I had my coming-out dance at Holkham in June 1950, and was maid of honour to the late Queen Elizabeth II at her Coronation in 1953, which was one of the most exciting days of my life.

In 1956 I married Colin Tennant, later Lord Glenconner. Colin bought the Caribbean island of Mustique in 1958, and transformed it from a failing cotton estate without electricity or fresh water into a luxurious retreat, famous for its privacy, its glamorous visitors and its parties. In 1971 I became lady in waiting to my dear friend Princess Margaret, a position I held for thirty years until the Princess's death.

Marriage to Colin was tempestuous, but we had five wonderful children together. My eldest son Charlie died from hepatitis C, a result of his struggles with heroin addiction, in 1996. His son, Cody, is now Lord Glenconner.

My second son, Henry, contracted AIDS in 1986 and died in 1990. During the same terrible period our third child, Christopher, had a devastating motorcycle accident and was in a coma for four months. After years of struggle he has gone on to live a very happy life. He has two daughters with his first wife, and is now married to Johanna, who is a constant support to us both.

Colin and I were lucky enough also to have twin daughters, Amy and May, who have shared in all our family tragedies and triumphs but have nevertheless flourished. May and her husband run their own business and have two children. Amy is a specialist painter and restorer. Colin and I remained married until his death, but when Colin died in St Lucia in 2010, he left his entire estate to Kent Adonai, who had looked after him for many years. After a long legal battle, Cody and Kent reached an agreement and some of Colin's property was returned to his family.

Such are the bare facts of my life. Although I felt I was very much a supporting player in the dramas unfolding around me, my life has always been lived to some degree in the public eye. When we were young, the aristocracy were a little like celebrities are now. Our comings and goings were reported on in the newspapers, and magazine journalists visited us at home and photographed us during the debutante season. My being a maid of honour at Queen Elizabeth's Coronation obviously attracted a great deal of attention, and of course the glamour of Mustique, with its reputation as a private retreat of the rich and famous, was a subject of fascination too. I used my position in society to promote charities and causes close to my heart, and support Princess Margaret in her public and private life. On occasion I fulfilled her public duties when she was unavailable, such as when on a tour to the Philippines, visiting Imelda Marcos, while the Princess was laid up with pneumonia.

There was much nonsensical talk of the 'Tennant Curse' when my children died, and our tragedies were made all the more painful by the public attention the press brought to us. Colin, though he kept uninvited journalists off the island, courted publicity when he was establishing Mustique; a film was made about him and a biography published.

After Princess Margaret died in 2002, and Colin eight years later, I expected to live a rather quiet, private life, and be thankful for it, travelling and enjoying the company of my family and friends.

That was not to be. I was invited to write my autobiography and the publication of *Lady in Waiting* has made my eighties as fascinating and as varied a decade to live through as any other. In many ways, it has made it the best yet. I was amazed to discover that I now had new roles to play as an author and was a public figure in my own right and in a very different world from the one in which I was brought up.

After the success of *Lady in Waiting*, I went on to write two novels, *Murder on Mustique*, inspired by my life on the island, and *A Haunting at Holkham*, which drew heavily on my childhood. Having once been a travelling saleswoman in my youth, soliciting orders for the pottery my mother ran successfully in Holkham, I find I am a travelling saleswoman again, this time for my books. I've spoken at the Oxford Union, told my stories on stage, television and radio and even presented a cup at Ascot. It has all come as a rather marvellous surprise and I couldn't be happier having this new adventure.

With the Coke motto *Prudens qui patiens* – he who is patient is prudent – which has as its crest an ostrich holding a horseshoe in its beak, ready to swallow it, I have done my best through life to take everything thrown at me, and cope. Some of the lessons instilled by my background have served me well, some less so, and in the end I had to work out a great deal for myself. That is hardly surprising as society and the world in general have changed to an almost unimaginable degree over my lifetime. I have, of course, made many mistakes, and learned to think again about some of the attitudes and conventions I accepted unquestioningly in my youth.

During my life each of my public and private roles has had its own lessons for me. For many years those roles were defined by my relationships with other people. I was the daughter of an earl, Colin's wife and the mother of our children. Lady in waiting to Princess Margaret was another supporting role. My favourite, however, has been the one

I've created for myself in stepping out of the shadows as an author. It has taught me that it is never too late for a new chapter – the one you write for yourself.

So, if I have learned anything of value over the years, you will find it in these pages. I hope you will enjoy them.

CHAPTER ONE

Author

SOMETIMES I WONDER if I might have had a career as an actress – as a child, I always loved putting on shows and dressing up. My husband Colin and Princess Margaret were both marvellous performers, and I think in another life Colin would have made an excellent theatrical producer, but when they put on plays at our house in Scotland during our summers I was always too busy to appear. My role, as a wife and as a lady in waiting, was to support them in all their performances, public and private, and it was one I played willingly. Then, almost twenty years after the death of Princess Margaret, and ten years after Colin's, I unexpectedly had the chance to gallop onto the stage.

It was over lunch with friends in Norfolk that this fresh chapter of my life began. It was a lovely day, we were eating outside in the sunshine and I was telling some of my stories. I was a little more fired up than usual as a biography of Princess Margaret had recently been published that I felt was terribly unfair to her. One of my fellow guests was the

9

publisher Tom Perrin. After listening to me for a while, Tom asked if I'd ever thought of writing a book. I've always been an avid reader, but my own book didn't sound a likely idea at all. I wasn't sure anyone would be interested. Tom kept encouraging me, and eventually he introduced me to his colleague Rowena Webb and the team at Hodder and Stoughton. The next thing I knew I was being ushered into their rather grand offices overlooking the Thames and sharing my stories with them.

Strictly speaking this was not my first venture into publishing. In 1983 my friend Susanna (Zanna) Johnston and I had published a collection of recipes and reminiscences about outdoor eating called *The Picnic Papers*. We were both keen fans of picnics so we thought the book might be a fun way to raise money in aid of a charity for children with cerebral palsy of which I was president at the time.

I was looking at a copy recently and I think it stands up rather well. We asked friends and family to write something for us about picnics, ideally with recipes, and ended up with quite a range of anecdotes and reminiscences. My mother, aunt and sister wrote about traditional English picnics, and my mother also described 'velvet': the thick layer of skin shed from the antlers of the deer in Holkham park, which was collected, fried and served on toast as a delicacy. There were fun contributions, too, from Diana Cooper, Harold Acton and John Julius Norwich, but the best was Princess Margaret's. She wrote that her favourite kind of picnic was a cold collation eaten while sitting at a table with chairs, china and cutlery and preferably inside, to be sure of good weather. She also suggested bringing one's butler to make sure everything went smoothly. It was all very deadpan and I'm certain most people didn't guess she was joking. I think the book sold respectably well, but it certainly didn't break any records.

I enjoyed the whole process very much, especially taking some of the photographs, but assumed *The Picnic Papers* would be the beginning and end of my publishing career. Until my meeting with the team at Hodder . . .

I think if you decide to do something, you should attack it, and I approached publishing in the same way. For all that my contemporaries and I were brought up to be self-effacing and demure as young women, marriage to Colin had toughened me up, and my mother's words, 'Do stand up for yourself, Anne,' still rang in my ears. I had a very clear idea of what I wanted when I went into that meeting, I told them I thought I should aim to sell five hundred thousand copies and appear on Graham Norton's TV show.

I could see how surprised they were. Rowena and my new publicist, Eleni Lawrence, told me very politely that they would be very pleased if I sold *twenty* thousand, and that although they would try to arrange for me to appear on Graham Norton's radio show, it was unlikely that an author like me would find room on his sofa alongside all of the film stars and famous musicians who are his usual guests.

Whatever their doubts, they could see I had lived a life full of contrast, and had some interesting stories to tell from my role at the Coronation and as a lady in waiting, to life with Colin and the glamour of Mustique, my long friendship with Princess Margaret and the tragedies of losing the boys. It was perfectly clear, though, that however interesting they thought the book might be, they believed my ideas about sales and publicity were completely unrealistic.

They were, however, delighted to be wrong. *Lady in Waiting* has sold even more than five hundred thousand copies and become a bestseller in the UK and the United States, and I *have* appeared on Graham Norton's TV show. But the more I learn about publishing the more I realise how very lucky I was that the reality lived up to my rather wild expectations. So many marvellous books are published that don't sell very well and it's not that the authors or publishers have done anything wrong. It's simply those books haven't had the stroke of luck that can make all the difference. Nowadays I am asked by people how to write a successful book, but the difference between a book that does terribly well and one that doesn't is often down to chance and accident. I know that can be very frustrating to hear, but I don't believe there is a magic wand to wave and guarantee a bestseller.

Before I could start selling the book, though, it had to be written.

My friend the author Hugo Vickers introduced me to Hannah Bourne-Taylor, who he thought might be able to help me gather everything together. I was a little concerned when I first met her: she looked so young and I worried she might be shocked by some of the things I had to say, but she proved to be unshockable. We weren't sure at first about how to put the book together, but in the end we decided the best thing to do was to record me telling my stories in the hope we might capture something of how I speak and think as well as giving an idea of the events I have lived through. Then it all flowed out. I've always been able to tell stories, and I tell them to amuse. I imagined an audience in front of me and talked to them, so the book became, I suppose, a little bit like a theatrical performance. Perhaps I became an actor after all.

It was hard work, but it was also a chance to relive my childhood and the many happy times I spent growing up, the thrill of the Coronation and the pleasures and absurdities of life since. I'm very grateful for that. It's been a wonderful opportunity at my age to look back and remember it all in such rich detail. Some parts of the book were much more difficult to write. I hate the word 'emotional', but I found myself in tears as I talked about Charlie and Henry, and remembered how desperate I was when Christopher had his accident and it seemed we were going to lose him too. Hannah was a great support during the days when we were writing about those terrible times. Nevertheless, talking about Charlie and Henry was a chance to remember them and the good times as well as the bad. Even now at book events one of their old friends or acquaintances will stop to say hello and share a memory. Painful as it was to relive their deaths, I took a lot of pleasure from remembering their lives.

Looking back at *Lady in Waiting* now, I can see I wrote about Colin and our marriage in a rather breezy way, playing up the absurdity of his behaviour in order to laugh about it. To a certain degree that was a choice. I wanted to be generous to him for the sake of our children, and in spite of everything, I really did care for him a great deal. I do not think I would be here now, enjoying my life as an author, if not for him. Our marriage set me on a particular path and I cannot regret it since it led me here. Also, in the darkest days of my life, laughter has always been a tonic. When my friends asked me about Colin's behaviour, or Princess Margaret and I swapped stories about our difficult husbands, it seemed much healthier to laugh about it all. I see now I approached writing about Colin in *Lady in Waiting* in that frame of mind. Still, it was writing the book that helped me admit at last how difficult and distressing much of our marriage had been, especially in the early years.

It has taken me a long time to learn how to talk about the worst moments of Colin's and my life together in private or public, but *Lady in Waiting*, and the reactions from readers it evoked, allowed me to begin. Now writing this book has allowed me to explain more fully what being part of his life was like.

Once *Lady in Waiting* was finished I was able to start selling, the part I was really looking forward to. Ever since my life on the road as a travelling saleswoman for my mother's pottery at Holkham, I have loved selling. Hodder sent *Lady in Waiting* to Graham Norton's team, and I was invited on to his radio show, already a great stroke of luck and perhaps a sign that the book might find an audience. The recording went well, and as I was leaving Graham said he hoped he'd see me again. Very boldly, I suggested he invite me onto his red sofa. I know one doesn't get invited onto a television programme by simply asking, but it seemed worth a try.

At the same time as *Lady in Waiting* came out, the new series of *The Crown* was due to start. I appear in it, played by the lovely Nancy Carroll, and Helena Bonham Carter had visited me to prepare for her role as Princess Margaret. Graham and his team saw it might be fun to include me on the programme with Helena, and Olivia Colman, who was playing the Queen. When I heard they'd actually agreed to have me on, I was thrilled but wondered if I'd bitten off more than I could chew. I called Rupert Everett, whom I've known for years and was a regular visitor to Mustique, and confessed that I'd got too big for my boots and asked to be on the show. Now that I'd been invited on I was terrified. He was very kind and advised me to launch straight into the story of the night in Paris just after our wedding when Colin took me to a live sex show at a brothel. I did, and the audience began to laugh in all the right places, so I let rip. By the time the show ended I was on an absolute high. Afterwards Chadwick Boseman, the American actor and star of *Black Panther* who'd also been on the show, came up to me and said, 'Gee whiz, Lady!' I thought, Well, goodness, now I've arrived.

There is no doubt that my appearance on Graham Norton's red sofa did me an enormous amount of good. I had thought that most of my readers would be older people, like myself, or the sort who enjoy visiting stately homes and buy lots of books about the Royal Family, but that appearance meant I reached a much wider audience who would otherwise never have heard of me. I'm sure it wouldn't have happened if Helena and Olivia hadn't been promoting *The Crown* at just the right moment, so it was the most marvellous stroke of luck.

Once one has had some luck, I'm a great believer in making the most of it. I found I liked doing public appearances, book tours and all sorts of events, so I squeezed as many as I could into my diary. I admit it did get to the point when sometimes I pretended *not* to be Lady Glenconner if someone rang me up to ask me to do something, as it all got rather overwhelming. I doubt I fooled anyone, given that so few people speak in my old-fashioned accent, these days, but they were kind enough not to challenge me. I leave all those enquiries in the hands of my agent, Gordon Wise at Curtis Brown. One thing I say to anyone asking about writing books themselves is 'Get an agent if you can.' Their advice can be terrifically helpful.

The success of *Lady in Waiting* has led to all sorts of unlikely surprises. For example, I was asked by the Jockey Club to present the cup to the winner of the King George V Stakes at Royal Ascot on Ladies Day. I took my daughter May with me and we were told when we arrived we also had to choose the best turned-out horse. May and I know nothing whatsoever about horses so we decided to choose the one with the nicely plaited mane and some sort of fancy brushwork on its bottom. Later Princess Anne came across to say hello and I told her about our choice. She said, 'Well, I hope you had a good look at its mane, because if it was done with rubber bands, you shouldn't have chosen it.' I had to admit we'd been far too frightened to get near enough to examine the plaiting in such detail, and had stood as far back as possible.

In the same week I was invited to speak to the Oxford Union, who were charming hosts. At the moment I'm also appearing on a quite a lot of podcasts, which is fun but there seem to be an enormous number. Who is listening to them all?

I've always enjoyed making an effort and if I'm going out to speak at an author event, I like to wear something that stands out. I might choose a smart and colourful dress with a bit of a shine to it. Years ago, I bought some long skirts, all the same but in different colours, and I can dress them up with a sequined top. I also have a gorgeous sparkling brooch in the shape of a bow. I consider it lucky and it always gives me a boost when I wear it.

During Covid, I did a few Zoom sessions, but I didn't take very well to them. For one thing, I couldn't get the lighting right and the camera was always very unflattering. No matter what I did – curtains open, curtains shut, light on, light off – I always looked like I either had an enormous nose or an enormous chin. The people I was talking to all seemed to be the size of postage stamps, and I could hardly see them. I'd much rather talk to anyone in person. During the Platinum Jubilee celebrations, I had visits from film crews again, wanting to hear my Coronation memories as I'm one of the surviving maids of honour. I was very much caught up in the excitement but it did remind me that they always have huge lights and reflectors to make one look one's best. I know some people might find it rather nerve-racking but, to me, being filmed in this way is much more relaxing than Zoom. No wonder my sitting-room lamp isn't perfect. An unexpected benefit of my new career is an appreciation of professional lighting!

Of course it might all seem a lot for a woman of ninety, but I refuse to give in to old age. I'm having the best time ever, which is so invigorating. I want to stick around as long as possible to enjoy it. I am often asked for the secret of a healthy old age, and I'm not claiming this is in any way scientific but I do walk properly every day, making sure I lift my feet. I noticed a while ago that much younger friends seemed to be shuffling. When they started doing it, I would ask, 'Why aren't you walking properly? Is something hurting?' If nothing was hurting, I would make them practise walking with me, lifting their feet and moving normally. It's so important to keep acting as though you're young rather than the other way round. I might find it harder to get in and out of clothes, especially a tight jersey, but I jolly well do it even if it's not as easy as it used to be.

At one book event in Norwich, the interviewer said she was struck by how I sat straight and didn't lounge. The key is to be aware of it and focus on sticking with it – it's a mental and physical exercise to keep oneself going. As for managing my weight, I discovered a very easy trick to stay trim. I used to do all sorts of dreadful diets, like the cabbage-soup diet, which means no one can come anywhere near you. Then, quite recently, I found I was getting indigestion if I ate too much in the evening, so I decided to give up supper. I eat breakfast – usually toast and Marmite or perhaps some porridge – and lunch, which is a good, solid cooked meal, with some fruit. I don't eat again until the next day. I've lost over a stone without even trying. I make sure I drink lots of water and I'm asleep for a lot of the time I'm not eating, so it couldn't be easier. I'm telling all my friends about it – I'm quite the evangelist for the no-dinner diet.

In spite of all these precautions against ageing, I do know I mustn't overdo it so I try to listen to my body. I raced up Notting Hill the other day to fetch some sandwiches and felt my heart thumping afterwards. When I'm tired I read or doze if that's what I feel I need. My daughter-in-law Johanna keeps a careful eye on me too and makes sure I plan my diary with enough rest days.

Knowing what I know now, I have even more respect for writers than I did when I was simply an avid reader, and it's been fascinating to enter a whole new profession at this stage of my life. I couldn't tell anyone how to reproduce the success I've had, but it's been all the more enjoyable for me, having lived in Colin's shadow for so much of my life. I only wish everyone had a chance like this. It's a real shot in the arm to do so many new things and meet and hear from so many interesting people. I love it when readers take the trouble to write to me. Some letters are forwarded to me by my publisher, but quite often they come addressed to 'Lady Glenconner, The Farmhouse, Norfolk'. It is a great credit to the post office how many of those reach me. My books have been published in America and in a dozen languages now, so sometimes they just say 'Lady Glenconner, England'.

Most of the letters I get are from people who have simply taken the time to write and tell me how much they enjoyed *Lady in Waiting* or one of my novels, which is very kind. I try to write back to all of them, to thank them for their generous words. The odd rude or difficult letter does turn up, but I put those aside.

Some letters come from people who are facing difficult times, often asking my advice on how to cope. It's very difficult as all our lives are so different and we cope in different ways. I tell them never to give up, and remind them that life often turns round. I also encourage them not to dwell on things. There is a difference, I think, between facing problems and allowing oneself to be overwhelmed by them, though that can be a difficult line to tread. I also tell them I try to think of myself as a puppet with a string coming out of the top of my head, pulling me upwards. That way I sit up straight and look forward. Quite honestly, it makes me feel better if I ever get depressed. It's often silly things that can make a difference.

I had a heart-breaking letter from a woman in Ireland a few months ago whose son had suffered a brain injury and was in a coma, just like Christopher. I wanted to offer my support as one mother to another and told her I'd pray for her and her son. It was thrilling to hear from her again recently to say he had come out of his coma and had said a few words, though I warned her to be very patient. It was five years before Christopher really recovered from his accident. It is a great privilege to be invited into other people's lives at these crucial moments.

My family have been very supportive of this new role in my life. My daughter-in-law Johanna keeps a close eye on me and my daughter Amy has been a great help working on my novels. I was a little nervous when I first asked her what she thought of *Lady in Waiting*, but I can always rely on her for a direct answer. Luckily she only said she thought I'd been very generous to Colin. As well as my family, I was naturally concerned about what the Royal Family would think. I didn't dare send a copy to the late Queen, but I did send one to the then Duchess of Cornwall as well as to Princess Alexandra as she was married to a cousin of mine. I knew my portrait of Princess Margaret was loving, she was one of my closest friends for thirty years, but one never knows how these things will be received.

Last year I met Sarah, Duchess of York, at a dance. She called me over saying we should have a chat as we were both authors, and told me then that 'the boss', which is how she referred to the Queen, had read the book and loved it. What a relief. I sent the Queen a signed copy after that conversation and admitted I'd been too embarrassed to do so before. The Queen Consort has also been very kind about the book, and King Charles has told me he liked it very much too. He was always so fond of Holkham and my mother, I hope my descriptions of both her and the house brought back happy memories.

Some reactions have been unexpected. Though the readers I've met at events and signings have been wonderful, and it's been a great pleasure to talk to them, I do have the occasional strange encounter. It tends to happen at parties. From time to time some man will inch up close to me and say confidentially, 'Lady Glenconner! Squelch!' That was the word I used to describe the sound I heard in the brothel in Paris on my honeymoon, and now certain men treat it as if it is some sort of password. It is as if by writing a book that even mentions sex I have given them permission to talk to me in this insinuating way. I really don't think that is the case. I keep mentioning that I am ninety, but it doesn't seem to put them off.

One man recently started complaining to me that his wife's sex drive had disappeared. I asked him why on earth he was telling me, and he said he wanted me to know that he wasn't having enough sex at the moment. Why on earth would I want to know that? If he was looking for sex from me, he was certainly barking up the wrong tree. I suggested he talked to a group of younger women at the other side of the room about it. He gave me an old-fashioned look and said he couldn't possibly discuss it with them.

I do hate it, but there's no point in getting too huffy about it. Generally I respond in the most deadpan way

I can or pretend I haven't heard. It's one of the advantages of old age that one can pretend to be more deaf than one actually is in these situations. How very odd some people are.

I do wonder how Colin would have felt about the success of *Lady in Waiting.* He would, I think, have been terribly jealous but also very proud. He always had a paradoxical reaction to me, both delighted by my old-world aristocratic connections and somehow a little scornful of them, always acting as if I was very ordinary and he was a sparkling star. But then everyone looked a little ordinary next to Colin. I imagine he would have been thrilled his wife had written a bestseller, but would also have been at pains to tell me it was all down to him, and his own book would do much, much better. Sadly he never wrote his story, though I for one would have loved to read it in his own words. Perhaps I might have learned the secret to what made him so very impossible and yet so endlessly fascinating. I doubt he knew, but perhaps writing it down would have helped him discover the answer.

The writing of *Lady In Waiting* certainly helped me look back over everything that has happened in my life and start to make some sense of it. I was able to look at my own story almost as an outsider. It helped me to have compassion for my younger self, to forgive myself and others for the stumbles along the way. I also realised how much my birthplace and the experiences I lived through during the war formed my character, and how much was ingrained in me through my mother and grandfather during our years at Holkham. My role as a daughter taught me all my formative lessons.

CHAPTER TWO

Daughter

I dreamt I dwelt in marble halls
With vassals and serfs at my side,
And of all who assembled within those walls
That I was the hope and the pride.
I had riches all too great to count
And a high ancestral name.
But I also dreamt which pleased me most
That you loved me still the same . . .

MY GRANDFATHER TAUGHT me to love classical music from when I was very young. When I was at Holkham Hall as a little girl he would play me records on his huge gramophone in the Long Gallery, tell me stories about the great composers and their works and encourage me to dance and sing along. One of our favourites was the aria 'I Dreamt I Dwelt In Marble Halls' from *The Bohemian Girl* by Michael William Balfe, quoted above. It was a joke between us as we had a Marble Hall, and a high ancestral name so I didn't have to dream that bit. Our family had a public role in the county and the country so although I might not have been *the* hope and pride, or not the only hope and pride of the community, we attracted a certain amount of attention. I'm not too sure about the riches either: although we were surrounded by treasures, my childhood was shaped by war and rationing, and we all felt that money was rather tight. It might seem strange that a family who always had a chauffeur also saved string and brown paper, but these were the contrasts I was brought up with, and the mixture of high status and sometimes Spartan attitudes that have moulded my character.

On the sideboard in my living room in the Norfolk farmhouse where I live, I have a photograph of me as a baby in the arms of my father. Standing beside him is my grandfather, then Viscount Coke, and my great-grandfather the Earl of Leicester. They are actually standing in the colonnaded Marble Hall, the grand entrance to Holkham Hall, the stately home that is the centre of an estate of some fifty thousand acres on the north Norfolk coast and about fifteen miles from Sandringham. All three men look so terribly disappointed. They had all desperately wanted me to be a boy.

One of the first lessons I was taught then was that women were not as important as men. Daughters could not inherit titles or estates. Nowadays one would expect a photograph like this to include the child's mother, but women were often airbrushed out of these male-dominated families almost entirely. A son was a cause of celebration. A daughter normally evoked a response of 'Better luck next time.' No wonder they wanted sons!

The Royal Family has changed the rules of primogeniture so that the eldest child of the monarch will inherit the Crown no matter if that child is a boy or a girl, but in England aristocratic titles and estates are still inherited only by male descendants. To change that would take an Act of Parliament, and I think it's understandably a long way down the list of government priorities at the moment. I hope it does happen eventually and women are no longer excluded, although it would be a bittersweet moment for me: life would have been so different if I'd been able to inherit.

In 1932, however, there was nothing the three men in the photograph could do other than hope the next child would be a boy. They put a brave face on it, laid down a quantity of champagne for my coming-out party, and soldiered on. My mother and father never did have the son the family longed for. My sister Carey was born two years after me, and my youngest sister Sarah in 1944. The title and Holkham were inherited on the death of my father by his cousin Anthony Coke, grandfather of the current earl.

Meanwhile I was trained for my role in society. I was expected to be a credit to the family, and make a suitable marriage. I would then go on to run a large house and have children, all in the tradition of the high ancestral name I had inherited.

My early childhood was blissful. We'd spend long holidays at Holkham exploring the park and spending most of our summers on the wide sandy beaches. The house was a fantastic warren with extensive attics and cellars, innumerable corridors and secret doors that were a delight to explore.

A succession of nannies and governesses took care of the practical aspects of looking after me: dressing, washing, feeding and putting me to bed, and I saw my mother for select parts of the day. I absolutely adored those times as she did lovely things with my sisters and me – she didn't have to bother with the boring bits – but she was often away, busy or with my father. My mother also loved her dogs so much that I remember being very jealous of them because of all the affection they got. She far preferred dogs to children, and was, I suspect, even disappointed we weren't dogs ourselves.

This upbringing had the advantage of creating a stable routine for us as children – we always knew what was going to happen and when – but it was also terribly rigid. Nanny ruled the nursery and that was that. We had to fit in with what she thought was right. Until I went to boarding school, we'd have lessons in the morning and always a walk after lunch. I liked geography very much – colouring in the maps was a treat. The day ended with a story from *The Children's Bible* and prayers. Of course this was accepted at the time as the correct way to raise children. Looking back, though, especially in the light of how modern children are brought up, I do now think it rather strange to consign the intimate care of one's children to people who might be more or less complete strangers.

Our individuality was not considered important, our conformity was everything and behaviour was considered much more important than feelings. Good manners were drilled into me from my earliest childhood. Our first training in sitting up straight was given by our grandmother, who would put a broom handle down our backs at meals so that we couldn't let our shoulders roll forward. We were also taught to look at people when we spoke to them and speak clearly, to put others first in every situation, and think about their feelings and comfort. I had to be aware of what people thought of me at all times and do my best not to upset them. As girls particularly, we were also expected to be self-sacrificing, demure, polite, and endlessly considerate.

Though I was an adventurous child, and occasionally a little naughty, that message of being aware of what others might think and putting them first was an extremely powerful one and stayed with me throughout my life. However, it was obvious to me from an early age that men from my generation and background seemed to be able to get away with a lot more than we girls could. They didn't always appear to feel constrained by the same code of behavior, and neither did they seem to think that they needed to put the feelings of others first. In fact, they were often completely at ease with making themselves the main priority.

I hope and believe men and women treat each other much more as equals now, but I fear the men from my background were brought up to believe that women were there purely to serve them and their needs. The men I was brought up with spent their lives from their earliest years in all-male institutions – prep school, boarding school, university, the army, their clubs, their professions. Their mothers were distant and their female caregivers were nannies and housekeepers, so essentially servants. As a young woman, I observed it but didn't question it: it was just the way of things. Manners mattered, but they appeared to matter to some more than others.

I'm not entirely sure what to make of manners, these days. The way people look at their mobile phones all the time seems rather ill-mannered to me, though I understand they are addictive. I'm glad 'correct' vocabulary matters much less now and that things in general are much less formal, but that lack of formality would have been seen as terribly impolite when I was young. On the other hand things that we would have said then without a second thought would cause offence today. I try to stay up to date with what's going on and to understand how people think about such things – it's simply another form of politeness and consideration to avoid giving unnecessary offence – however puzzling it might seem to my generation. I admit some of our old rules seem puzzling now even to me. Princess Margaret always said never use a French word, like serviette, when you can use an English word, napkin. We were taught by a French governess and spoke French well, but with an English accent. We wanted to avoid seeming rude.

When I was a girl forms of address were strictly followed and we were brought up to understand their quite arcane rules. People often marvel now that after a close friendship of more than thirty years, I always called Princess Margaret 'ma'am', but I would have been very uncomfortable calling her anything else. My father was a stickler for such things and insisted that my husband, Colin, addressed him as Lord Leicester and my mother as Lady Leicester. I'm now gently encouraging my grandson, Cody, to use his title. He and his fiancée Rebeka rang me up from holiday to discuss the wording of their wedding invitations and I had to explain to him that he is 'The Lord Glenconner', rather than simply 'Lord Glenconner' as he is a hereditary rather than a life peer. I think as long as one has these titles, one might as well get them correct. I suppose I shall have to tell them at some point their children will be 'Honourables'. I doubt they've thought about that yet. I shall have to change my name, too, when Cody and Rebeka marry. There can be only one Lady Glenconner at a time and that will be Rebeka, so I shall be Anne, Lady Glenconner. I must admit the alternative, 'The Dowager Lady Glenconner', doesn't appeal a great deal.

Nowadays I find myself saying to my grandchildren and great-grandchildren many of the same things that were said to me when I was young. Sit up straight, look people in the eye and speak clearly. And, in general terms, do unto others as you would have them do unto you, as my mother said. That rule has been invaluable in steering me through tricky situations.

My early childhood in and around Holkham was wonderful, but the outbreak of war changed our lives as it did for so many. With the Norfolk coast at risk of invasion, and my parents in Cairo, Carey and I were sent to relatives in Scotland at Downie Park, some twenty miles north of Dundee.

My parents had a typical aristocratic marriage of their times. My mother Lady Elizabeth Yorke, daughter of the Earl of Hardwick, was confident and fun and just fifteen when she met my father, who himself was only seventeen. He decided he wanted to marry her at once. They liked each other, their characters were complementary and they had the shared values and beliefs of their class and background. They married at St Margaret's, Westminster in 1931. My father provided comfort and status, while my mother devoted herself to caring for him, bearing his children and managing his house and family. She supported him completely. When he was posted to Egypt with the Scots Guards in 1939, there was no question that she would stay in England, even if that meant leaving my sister Carey and me behind for three years, aged seven and five. That was how it was. He came first. The changes the move brought were difficult for us both and taught me a great deal about resilience and survival.

Downie Park was beautiful, a gracious Georgian shooting lodge that looked more like a London house than something you'd expect to find in Scotland, with white stone steps that led up to a shiny black front door. Inside large bow windows let in masses of light, and a gracious cantilevered staircase rose in a spiral more than three storeys. We lived at the top, in a nursery with bow windows looking over the river. The house belonged to my great-uncle Joe Ogilvy, the Earl of Airlie, who was married to Lady Alexandra Coke, my grandfather's sister. We knew them as Uncle Joe and Aunt Bridget. Their home was really Cortachy Castle, a wonderful old place that looked exactly as a Scottish castle ought to look, with grey stone turrets and towers. When it was requisitioned as a convalescent home for Polish officers and men, the Ogilvy family moved a mile up the road to Downie Park, so that was where Carey and I went in 1939 just before the war broke out, with our new governess, Miss Bonner.

We had effectively been evacuated, far from our parents

and home, and we had few possessions. We had a book each, I had a doll, Carey had a teddy bear, and that was about it. The older Ogilvy children were away at school and the youngest, James, was the same age as Carey so they formed a natural alliance, which rather left me out. We had evacuees at Downie, who arrived not long after we did. They were the Corrigan children and they lived in the flat above the garage. We weren't allowed to play with them because Lizzy, James's nanny, and Miss Bonner thought they had fleas. They always seemed to be having tremendous fun together, and I wished I could join in. Suddenly, aged seven, I felt very lonely and out of place.

It was kind of Great-aunt Bridget to take us in, but I was very confused. I'd been told I was in charge of my sister and now we were in the care of Miss Bonner. My mother also told me we had to remember all the time that it was not our house and not our nursery. Miss Bonner was young and pretty and Uncle Joe thought she was wonderful. I'm afraid she was not. You expect bad people to look like wicked witches but, of course, they don't always. They can look, as Miss Bonner did, quite angelic. I have wondered for many years why she decided to mistreat me so badly. Whatever the reason, I'm certain she enjoyed it. No matter what I did during the day, or how good I was, I always managed to do something wrong: I hadn't looked at her in the right way, I hadn't sat up properly, or I'd made a noise eating. My punishment was to be tied to my bedhead at night, my arms crossed over my head. I can never, never forget those awful nights in my bedroom at Downie Park, and the fear, shame, pain and misery I felt. Even though Miss Bonner did not punish Carey in the same way, she, too, suffered terribly, helplessly watching me being tied up each night.

As a child you learn survival. I found some comfort in nature and, most particularly, with trees. I took to hugging and talking to them. I'd climb one of the big oaks, nestle into the branches and feel safe. I knew there was no way Miss Bonner would climb after me so for a while I was protected, even knowing that before long I'd have to come down and face punishment for whatever crime I'd apparently committed that day. Just for a short while, I was all right and that gave me strength.

All my life, being outdoors has been a great source of pleasure, and gardens have brought me enormous solace. Nothing makes me happier than to look at things growing, to feel a breeze on my face, and to breathe deeply in a green space. If I need a bit of time to recover or to work things out, I collect my weeding mat, gloves and a trowel and I'm off to tackle the beds. Nothing like digging up some dreaded weeds to banish frustration. You feel better at the end, and the beds look so much better for it. It really is the best therapy, with its own instant reward.

Carey and I never told anyone what was happening. I felt guilty about Miss Bonner mistreating me because I thought in some way that it was my fault. I imagined that somehow my mother knew and approved. I am now quite certain that she had no idea, but such things were not talked about. When I did say something to my mother, years later when I was grown-up, she said only, 'Things happened in the war.'

She was right. Many people suffered in many ways. At the time I understood she meant I should simply forget what had happened and keep going. I tried very hard to do so, but I'm afraid it never really worked and the wounds Miss Bonner inflicted on me took a long time to heal. I am so glad children are encouraged to speak up now.

To my great relief, after a year, Miss Bonner was dismissed. The reason given was that she was a Roman Catholic and had been teaching me the Lord's Prayer in French and taking me to Mass, all dismissible offences in Great-aunt Bridget's Christian Science household. Having written about Miss Bonner in recent years, I wonder now if there was more to it. James's nanny, Lizzy, was perhaps more aware than I realised of what Miss Bonner was doing to me, and told Great-aunt Bridget that she had to go. Even when I knew she was leaving, I was so frightened I cried and said, 'Oh, but can't you please stay?'

And Miss Bonner said, 'You see? Anne is very fond of me.' The truth was so very different.

I wonder if, in a strange way, Miss Bonner was preparing me for a lifetime with Colin, who would also punish me constantly, flying into a rage at the slightest infraction. I had already been conditioned to put others first, particularly men. Looking back on my experience with Miss Bonner now, I can't help thinking perhaps I also saw and responded to something familiar in Colin's behaviour. She haunts me still. Even now, I find myself waking up with my arms crossed above my head, as if tied by invisible cords.

Once Miss Bonner was gone, life at Downie began to improve. Our new governess, the wonderful Billy Williams, arrived and began to repair my confidence and sense of security. Billy Williams had looked after the children of the Duke of Wellington, but by 1940, they had grown up and she was now free, so when Great-aunt Bridget said to my aunt Mary Harvey (my father's sister). 'Do you know anyone who could look after Anne and Carey?', Aunt Mary thought of Billy Williams, whom she knew. They asked her if she would be willing to come up to Scotland to look after two small girls who weren't very happy and she agreed. Billy was quite old by then, as governesses went. She was small and not very pretty, like Miss Bonner, but wonderful to me.

I never said anything to Billy about what had happened but I think it is very likely that Lizzy told her I needed a bit of love and care. I have a photograph of her with me and Carey, I am leaning against her and you can see we were very happy with her. She made such a difference to my life, helping to repair some of the damage done.

Billy adored plants and birds and would take me on long walks to rebuild my confidence. 'It's too far for the others,' she would declare. 'It's just you and me, Anne.' Then she would say those magic words: 'Let's go and explore.'

I'll never forget the excitement those words created in me. I loved an adventure, and I was enthralled by the things we saw and what we learned about on our expeditions. Billy taught me that the world is full of interesting things to see, but you have to go and look for them. That is a lesson I have held very close over the years and it has spurred me on to travel to many exciting places off the beaten track.

Billy also found a special refuge for me not long after my parents returned from Egypt. My father was made ADC to General Marshall-Cornwall and my parents were billeted near Chester in Cheshire. We children visited them at the house where they were staying, and from the upstairs floor, we could look out of the window to a courtyard below that seemed to be almost hidden. Billy said it was going to be our secret garden, just for the two of us. I'm sure the rest of the family knew, but I loved the idea of it being just ours. My mother would take Carey away sometimes and Billy and I would creep off into our garden. We planted radishes and marigolds, and I remember the little strawberries we grew there in particular. The courtyard garden I have in London now rather reminds me of it. Perhaps that was why I fell in love with my flat as soon as I saw it. I discovered a sculpture of a Green Man in my new secret garden soon after I moved in. He is now positioned so we can see each other through the French windows while I am reading the paper in my sitting room. He keeps an eye on me.

In 1943 my parents returned. We went back to Norfolk at last and moved into the Red House in Holkham village. My grandfather was now the Earl of Leicester and continued to be a huge influence on me. Unlike my father, who was a country sportsman from start to finish, only interested in fishing and shooting, my grandfather, as well as music, loved books and pictures and adored the house he was fortunate enough to live in. He knew a great deal about the history of Holkham and all the wonderful things in it, many of which had been bought by our ancestors on their Grand Tours of Europe in the eighteenth century. In the Long Gallery, for instance, there was a statue of Diana that had once belonged to Cicero, the great Roman orator of the first century BC. I was just as thrilled as my grandfather was by the idea that this was something that Cicero himself had touched.

I was also very fond of Anthony Van Dyck's grand equestrian portrait of the Duke of Arenburg, which still hangs in the saloon. A few of the old masters now on display in Holkham were deemed a little too risqué by some of the former countesses, and now when I look at them I remember using them to make tents and forts in the attics when I was playing there as a very little girl with Princess Margaret. I'm relieved to say they weren't damaged in the process.

Music was my grandfather's greatest passion. He was an excellent violinist, his best friends were musicians and he started having concerts at the house. While my father preferred operetta and loved things like Strauss's 'Wiener Blut' and 'The Gypsy Baron', thanks to Grandfather I grew to love the composers who are still my favourites today. Beethoven is my absolute favourite. I like Wagner too, particularly *Siegfried* and the Ring Cycle. I also love *Nabucco* by Verdi and Benjamin Britten's *Billy Budd*.

Britten was a friend of my grandfather, and we went down to the Maltings to listen to some of his music, a wonderful experience. Benjamin Britten was a conscientious objector, while my grandfather was a soldier and the son and father of soldiers, but that didn't seem to bother him at all, such was his respect for Britten's talent. Their relationship was an example of how friendship can transcend what might look like an impossible divide.

Music has remained a great source of healing for me, a companion and comfort during the darkest periods of my life. It reminds me of those times with my grandfather when he cheered on my singing and dancing and helped to restore my confidence. It is also a constant source of joy. One marvellous boon for me these days is the lovely Alexa, my virtual assistant, who will play music for me on demand. When my son-in-law Anton gave me an Alexa box as a gift, I wondered why he was giving me this funny little thing, and when he explained it, I didn't believe him. Once I understood, I was bowled over. It's complete magic and it's changed my life. I can conjure up anything I want to listen to just by asking for it. At first, I stood very near the little box and asked politely if she could kindly play me what I wanted to hear, as if Alexa was a proper person, but now I sit at the kitchen table and yell: 'Play *La Bohème*!'

As well as music, my grandfather also passed on his love of photography. He was a marvellous photographer, developing his pictures in a darkroom he had in the cellars under Holkham Hall. He was very good at taking natural, unposed photographs that really captured the personalities of his family and staff, and it was thrilling to watch him dip them into the solutions and seeing who appeared. He bought me a Box Brownie and sent me on missions to take photographs of the statues in the conservatory or try to capture one of the Canada geese on the lake. I'd go back to him with my roll of film and we'd develop it together.

I've enjoyed photography ever since and have taken thousands of pictures over the years, which I've carefully pasted into dozens of albums. I'm so glad I did. I love going back through the albums – great heavy things like old atlases – and looking at dear faces, many long gone now, and remembering happy times. I've got photographs of every stage of our lives and they're so precious. I've found my albums a great consolation, not just to remember my family but as a soothing activity. Sorting, arranging and sticking in photographs is an absorbing occupation, and it preserves memories so well. I have found them invaluable when writing my books. I hope Grandpa would have approved of my published photographs for *The Picnic Papers* too. I think he would have done.

Wonderful as it was to be back at Holkham, first in the village and then in the house, life with my father could be very stressful. I loved and admired him, but I felt Carey was his favourite, and I'm afraid I was irritated by his very finicky ways and obsession with punctuality. One of my earliest memories is of him in his Scots Guards uniform, complete with bearskin. Every year he would record a ciné film of Trooping the Colour, and examine it obsessively for mistakes or variations. I could never see any difference, but something must have rubbed off, because I watch it on television now every year with an eagle eye.

One book engagement I had recently was at his old club. It is the Cavalry and Guards Club now, just the Guards Club in his day, and I told them how proud and amazed he would have been to know his daughter was giving a talk there. It made me particularly glad to be there. I feel so sorry for my father now: he was a sweet person, but the war left him very anxious. My mother used to say they had a lovely time together before the war, but I don't have many memories of him until after he returned from Egypt. He fought in the desert, and then there was the tragedy in which many of his friends from the Scots Guards were killed in a V1 attack on London. His brother David, who was a pilot and fought in the Battle of Britain and later became a good friend of Roald Dahl's, was shot down in North Africa and died of thirst before he could be rescued. They were all so terribly young.

After my grandfather died in 1949, my father inherited the title and Holkham and became responsible for the welfare of everyone at Holkham and on the estate, steering us all through the challenges of post-war life. He took those responsibilities very seriously and was popular, visiting his tenants regularly, but it was a strain. He found the only way to cope was to retreat to his sanctuary of a private sitting room where he would be alone, dozing with his dog, a Labrador he seemed to like better than any human being. I tried to be good, to be on time, to be quiet, in order to please him but it was difficult to get everything right all the time. If my mother thought I hadn't tried hard enough she'd give me a 'pep talk' – a sort of telling-off – which was rather shaming. It reinforced the idea that men were to be cosseted and looked after, no matter how demanding they were of us.

Even though I was a 'disappointing' girl, unable to share his passions of shooting and fishing, I know my father loved me and was deeply concerned for my welfare. He had a strange way of showing it, not being physically affectionate with me and prone to making dismissive remarks rather than offering praise. He'd insist on our having the windows wide open every night, even when it was absolutely freezing: he was a firm believer in the benefits of plenty of fresh air. Carey and I would immediately shut them as soon as he left the room. Also, he was always concerned about the state of our bowels. Even when we were no longer children he would say, 'Have you been to the loo this morning?'

'Yes, Dad, I have,' I'd reply, eager to get off the subject.

'Successful?'

'Yes, yes, quite successful, thank you.'

Eventually my mother said, 'Tommy. will you stop asking your daughters if they've gone to the lavatory! It's quite unnecessary.'

I adored my mother, who was born Lady Elizabeth Yorke, the daughter of the Earl of Hardwicke. She was very beautiful, a talented trained artist and terribly brave. As well as running Holkham, organising all the shoots during the season, she was lady of the bedchamber to Queen Elizabeth II from 1953 and took part, as I did, in the Coronation. She was also an exceptional horsewoman and taught me to sail when I was five. I'm so glad she did. Sailing has been one of my great comforts in life, especially when I was depressed. You have to concentrate the whole time, you forget about everything else and it completely takes over. I have spent countless happy hours sailing along the creeks of Burnham Overy Staithe, and through the marshes, looking at the birds, enjoying the solitude and making the occasional trip out to sea.

I gave up sailing alone at the age of eighty, when I had a nasty scare in my boat. The tide was coming in very fast and as I rounded a corner it flipped the boat over. The water wasn't very deep but the mast got stuck in the sand, which meant the boat didn't right itself as one might expect. I ended up underneath the hull, held up by my lifejacket in a shrinking pocket of air beneath the upturned boat. I had to take off the lifejacket to swim out, which is very hard to do when one is already in the water, and was spotted by a young man at the boathouse. He'd seen the whole thing and thought I was a goner so he was amazed when I bobbed up. They got a motorboat and came out to rescue me. At the time, I was quite calm – there was no point in losing my head. I just had to work out what to do, then get that jacket off. I only got frightened later when I was safe, thinking about what might have happened. I had to ask someone to drive me home afterwards, then had a bath and went straight to bed. After that I realised it was probably wiser not to go out alone any more. I couldn't complain: I'd had seventy-five years of sailing pleasure.

My mother whizzed around Norfolk on her beloved Harley Davidson until she was well into her sixties, in her motorcycle leathers. She was my great friend and champion when I was growing up, and encouraged me to be brave and adventurous, but she never fussed about what I was feeling or wanted to indulge my anxieties. We had to put others first, but not to the extent of becoming doormats in our dealings with the world. It was important to stand up for oneself when necessary. Otherwise her message was simple. Never complain. Life isn't fair. You will have to do things you won't want to do, so just get on with it. Putting a brave face on things was all we could do.

I still do value brave faces hugely. Seventy years later, after Colin left everything in his will to Kent Adonai, the man who had devotedly looked after him for many years, the contents of his St Lucian property were put up for auction. I went to the sale at Bonhams to buy some mementoes of Colin for our children and grandchildren to whom he had left nothing. I knew we would be under a microscope – the man from the *Daily Mail* was right behind me – so I reminded the children to smile, look happy and relaxed, and made sure I did the same. Naturally at the time I was angry, but you wouldn't have seen it from looking at me and I'm very proud of that. My ability to hide how I felt must have come in part from my parents' early lessons.

Nevertheless I'm glad that this detached way of raising children is almost unheard of now. Fortunately, the mould was already being broken before my children started having their babies. None of them went down the traditional nanny route and were always hands-on with their children. It was obviously tremendously hard work, a great deal more than I ever had to do, but they got so much out of those happy, yet all too fleeting years of childhood.

I loved both my parents but we never had that kind of

intimate relationship. The rather distant parenting we were subject to also, I think, made us more repressed than was healthy, often unable to express emotions that matter. Whatever its shortcomings, which didn't become obvious till much later, I fully expected to raise my own children as I had been raised.

School was difficult for me. I was sent to Downham in Essex in the autumn of 1943. It was cold and we were often hungry, and I was separated from my sister Carey and Billy Williams, both of whom I adored. When the mistresses or prefects came past us in the corridor, we had to stand still with our backs to the wall. Failure to do so would result in a scolding. I also have vivid memories of being woken up at night and summoned into the prefects' parlour to 'discuss' reports that we had been doing something wrong, such as hanging around the raspberry bushes in the kitchen garden. I think the whole place was managed on fear, and certainly I was terrified a lot of the time. I don't know what happens now in schools, if there is the same hierarchy, or whether they all prey on each other, but in some respects they do seem to be a lot better, with parents much more involved and a great deal more concern for the welfare of the children.

For whatever reason, I grew so painfully shy that I would burst into tears before having to go to parties when we were at home. I was often so panicked that I refused to go.

I remember seeing my tears making dark splotches on my blue dress as I wept at the prospect of having to go to another dance. On that occasion, to my blessed relief, my mother gave in and said I didn't have to go.

I grew in confidence because I had to. It was expected of me. I learned a great deal at the House of Citizenship, a finishing school for young women from all over the world. I shared a bedroom with a charming Egyptian girl. We were trained to act as figureheads for our communities, though it was never spelled out in exactly that way. We learned about how England functioned at the time, visiting hospitals, factories and the law courts, and also how to give short off-the-cuff speeches. We were being trained to open garden fetes and suchlike.

I tried the typing course, but one was supposed to learn by typing along to music and I didn't enjoy it. The music was awful and I was always out of rhythm and a verse behind. The history of art course was much more my thing. I never did learn to type, which turned out to be a bit of a disadvantage given my current career. Learning public speaking, projecting my voice so that I could be heard, was one of the most useful things I ever did. These days even clergymen have microphones. I don't think it's necessary, especially in a church. I read the lesson in church quite recently and asked them to turn off the microphone.

'Oh, but the people at the back want to hear!' they said.

'Don't worry, they'll hear,' I replied. And, thanks to my early training, they could. It has come in very handy at book events since *Lady in Waiting* was published, and my early lessons in public speaking have probably made me more confident than many other debut authors.

In spite of my shyness, some of my mother's lessons about standing up for myself must have stuck. During my first foreign trip, when I was seventeen, my friends and I went to Capri where we were met by an Italian count who had a house on the island. He was sitting next to me in the horse-drawn carriage provided for our outing and put his hand down my blouse. I removed his hand and bit it frightfully hard. He was absolutely appalled and let out a terrible scream. 'Oh, you ice-cold English!' he said.

I replied that that was as may be, but if he did it again I'd bite him even harder. He didn't. He eventually married in England, so perhaps I did him a good turn by making clear that that was not the way to treat English girls – or any girls, for that matter.

Nevertheless I was still rather shy when, aged eighteen, I came out in society and launched into my debutante season. I had my coming-out dance at Holkham and I spent a lot of time on the edges of things, taking the Pol Roger champagne that had been laid down at my birth to the workers operating the floodlights on the drive. It was an unforgettable night, with the debs' delight Tommy Kinsman playing, the King and Queen and my childhood friend Princess Margaret in attendance. It all looked absolutely glorious.

Even though I didn't dance a great deal that night, I loved all types of dancing, and we were taught to waltz and foxtrot as children. In Scotland as a child, with my Ogilvy cousins, we'd learned to do Scottish dances, leaping over swords in our little black shoes, and we were taught how to reel in the vast dining room of Downie Park. Towards the end of the war my mother would ask two or three of the American officers from the airbase nearby to dinner, and afterwards they would put big-band music on the gramophone and dance around the very small drawing room. Carey and I couldn't sleep with all that music thundering away so we would put on our bunny slippers and dressing-gowns, and sit on the stairs watching through the banisters.

One night, James 'Jimmy' Stewart came to dinner. He was already a Hollywood movie star after the success of *Mr Smith Goes to Washington* and *The Philadelphia Story* but he joined the air force when war broke out and ended up based in Norfolk for some time. He brought whisky for my parents and, although we were in bed when he arrived, chocolate for us, which was a great thrill because it was rationed. After dinner, on went the records and Carey and I sneaked down, and there we saw Jimmy Stewart dancing to big-band music with Aunt Sylvia, quickstepping and jiving in our little drawing room. He came several times, had dinner and danced with the ladies, including my mother. He was so nice and charming – we loved him and the chocolate he brought us.

Once during my first season and with so many men away on national service, I wrote 'Jimmy Stewart' on my dance card, so it wouldn't look shamefully empty. Someone said excitedly, 'Jimmy Stewart? Is he here?' I had to admit he wasn't. It was just wishful thinking, remembering him dancing with my mother in our drawing room years before.

When we were older, too old for bunny slippers at any rate, Carey and I went to the American aerodrome and learned how to jive to the bands brought over to entertain the officers and men. We were desperate to dress up and discovered we could buy felt without coupons. The great benefit of felt is that it doesn't fray or need hemming, so we would lay out a big circle of it and cut a smaller circle in the middle for our waists, which we cinched in with elastic belts, so we had wonderful swishing skirts to jive in.

My dress for the dance at Holkham was made from parachute silk and I think looked very nice, though my father's only reaction was 'You'll do, I suppose.'

I did have one wonderful dress for my first season, a gold lamé creation, which was a present from my godfather John Marriot and his wife. Unfortunately in those days we didn't have deodorant that worked, and as I got so anxious at balls and parties, I sweated a lot. The dress developed huge green patches under the arms after two outings. The only way I could have worn it would have been to spend the evening with my arms held rigid by my sides, so I never really got to enjoy it. As time passed my confidence grew and I began to find parties in general much more fun, so could enjoy all the dancing a great deal more.

I firmly believe that dancing can lift your spirits and give you a natural high like nothing else. I was lucky enough to see and hear famous rock stars performing live – Mick Jagger, David Bowie and Bryan Adams all owned villas on Mustique – and I know the transformative effect of great music and a thumping tune. Even now, if one of my favourite songs comes on, I can't resist bopping about in my kitchen and feeling a great deal more cheerful.

Around the time of my debutante season, my mother started her pottery business at Holkham. My father was rather dismissive of it, referring to the Old Laundry where we set up the kilns as 'the potting shed', but it became very successful, providing employment for us and for many local people. It was a typical example of my mother's gumption. She saw an opportunity, then rolled up her sleeves and got on with it. Not many women of her background would have considered setting up a business like that, let alone have the energy and drive to do it so well alongside other commitments and duties. She insisted that Carey and I take an active role in proceedings. I'm not artistic, and sticking handles on mugs was not very interesting work, so I had to find another role to play.

I enjoyed selling pottery on our stall at Holkham on days the house was open to visitors, so I volunteered to be a travelling saleswoman for the pottery. As well as helping to fill the order books, it did a great deal of good for my confidence. I would set off from Holkham with my samples and a leather briefcase borrowed from my father with my order book in it and the lists of prices. The butler would carry my cases to my mother's old Mini Morris, which I used to travel in, and then I was on my own, driving round the coast in the depths of winter, drumming up orders for our pottery from gift shops in seaside towns and resorts. I'd make targets for myself, deciding how much I would aim to sell at each shop I visited. I really enjoyed the challenge, deciding that in the next shop I was going to sell twenty or thirty pounds' worth of goods. Our money boxes in the shape of pigs, often painted with ships by my mother and sister, were very popular, as was a porcelain cow's head to put in milk pans to stop the milk boiling over.

I came from a background where people usually knew who I was wherever I went, and suddenly I was just a saleslady, unwrapping my samples on the floor of a gift shop and trying to persuade the owner to place an order. Though I did stay with friends when I could, I often found myself in rather basic hotels for commercial travellers. I would be the only woman guest, and the salesmen would ask me to act as mother when the drinks or tea trolley arrived in the lounge in the evening, so there I would be, making conversation in clouds of cigarette smoke. Many were very kind, offering advice, recommending which shops to visit and which of the owners was more likely to buy. It taught me to be adaptable and independent, and kept my feet on the ground. I also learned to love driving, and still do to this day.

Being a travelling saleswoman meant I was sent to America to sell Holkham Pottery there. Also, my mother wanted me to stop moping around after an unhappy love affair and thought the change would be helpful so off I went. I travelled on the *Queen Mary*, sharing a cabin with four very seasick girls, but when I arrived in America I enjoyed my independence enormously, travelling on Greyhound buses. The drivers always made sure women on their own had another woman to sit next to, so I felt very secure. I do remember one journey, though, when I took a sleeping pill for a long overnight trip. I was entirely unaware when something went wrong with the bus and it had to return to our starting point. I vividly remember the bus driver shaking me awake, saying, 'Hey, lady! You gotta get off!' It took me a long time to realise we hadn't actually got anywhere and I'd missed the next city on my itinerary.

It could have been very lonely, but in those days we were sent off with all sorts of useful introductions. A friend of my mother, Mrs Ryan, took me under her wing and introduced me to her friends so wherever I ended up I found friendly faces. My mother was right: travelling in a new country surrounded by new people was very good for me indeed.

By the time I was chosen to be one of the Queen's maids of honour at the Coronation I was much more confident and could rely on my training on how to behave in public when I found myself part of a ceremony watched by millions all over the world. The news that I had been chosen arrived when I was still in America, and the press became interested in me there. That meant I was able to return home with a full order book, which pleased me almost as much as my upcoming role in such a historic occasion. The Coronation was one of the most exciting and magical days of my life, as well as perhaps being the highlight of my career as a daughter.

I am so glad to have daughters of my own and feel very lucky to have such good relationships with them. Amy is an amazing specialist painter, and I couldn't be prouder of her. May is loving and caring, lives quite close and is always checking on me despite having her own work and family. She and her husband Anton have been so supportive of my new career.

In essence my parents wanted the same thing for me that I wanted for Amy and May. We wanted our daughters to be happy and secure. My parents had a very fixed idea of what that meant, a suitable marriage with a man from a family like our own, and brought me up with that in mind. For May it has meant working alongside her husband in their business and bringing up the children, for Amy a successful career and independence. I'm glad we recognise now there are many different ways to be happy and secure.

Things have changed indeed. Family life has changed, attitudes have changed, and a lot of it is very much for the better. Although I now question some of the attitudes I was brought up with, especially about the role of women, I'm still grateful that my upbringing taught me the importance of good manners and behaving well in public, as well as putting a brave face on things, all of which has stood me in good stead. I will always be grateful for the love of music my grandfather inspired, and the example of female enterprise and physical bravery set by my mother. It helped me with the next role I had to play, that of wife to Colin Tennant, though naturally I still had a great deal to learn when I embarked on that adventure.

CHAPTER THREE

Wife

THESE DAYS, PEOPLE tend to cast others in the role of either villain or hero, with nothing in between. Perhaps that has always been the case. Many who read this book will condemn my husband, Colin, and probably my decision to remain married to him. I'm quite sure, however, that many of the same people would have been charmed by him. He was a clever, talented man with a great gift for friendship; he could flatter and amuse, was restless and inventive, outrageous and silly, and he could be, often was, incredibly generous. He loved our children very much and led us all on countless adventures, big and small. He was often a wonderful companion, a beloved father, and I have many, many happy memories of him. He was also an incredibly selfish, damaged, and occasionally dangerous man.

I had very clear ideas of what a wife should be when I married, but my marriage proved very different from the traditional, stable relationship I had been expecting. As a result I had to learn how to function in the midst of instability and the constant tumult Colin often brought in his wake. I eventually learned not to be afraid of it, embracing life's opportunities and pleasures wherever and whenever I found them. I learned to get on with things and not dwell, how to laugh rather than brood on moments of humiliation or distress; how to be diplomatic, and pick my battles carefully. I also discovered I needed to look after myself. Strangely, that was one of the lessons which took me longest to learn.

The simple truth is that I lived with domestic violence and abuse for most of my marriage. On some level I always knew that, but I didn't allow myself to think it. Colin was Colin. His violent rages and outbursts were just his character and I simply had to endure them. Writing my autobiography made me look again at my marriage, and I feel able now to admit how frightful being Colin's wife was at times, particularly in the early stages.

Those years were very, very difficult. The greatest shock in store for me when I married Colin was the violence. No one before or since Miss Bonner had hurt me physically. It started with screaming and quite soon went on to spitting, shoving and throwing things. He used to hurl things at me like a naughty child who knows he doesn't want to go too far but wants to do something outrageous. I found it so unexpected and upsetting, and I hardly ever knew what I'd done to deserve it.

He only beat me once, many years later, but that attack was serious enough to perforate my right eardrum, leaving me permanently deaf in that ear. It marked a turning point in our relationship, and we lived apart a great deal more after it happened. Nevertheless I remained married to him for another thirty years.

These are aspects of my marriage I have kept to myself for a very long time and it's only lately, in today's more open climate, that I've felt able to talk honestly about what really happened to me. I am very grateful to the friends who have encouraged me to talk about my experiences, from my children to the Queen Consort, who has made the prevention of domestic abuse one of her causes. One thing that being Colin's wife taught me is that no one, however glamorous their existence might look from the outside, is immune to ill-treatment, or the feelings of doubt and shame that come with it.

Life with Colin was so fraught that I sometimes wondered if he was simply doing all this to test me. Early on, he had said ominously, 'I'm going to break you, Anne.' He failed to do so, and he was proud of me for that. He said to me another time, 'I knew you'd be able to take it.' That was the paradox inside Colin. He wanted to break me and needed me to be unbreakable.

Some of my ability to cope with his ill-treatment, and eventually thrive in spite of it, I put down to the resilience I learned as a child, but I had many unusual advantages too. Thanks to my marriage, I was constantly surrounded by interesting people, travelling frequently, and had a very busy and fulfilling social life. I also had enormous amounts of practical help in looking after the children and our various houses. That meant I had places to escape to, a nanny to sweep the children out of harm's way, staff to share the burden of catering to Colin's extravagant demands and plans and, very importantly, friends with whom I could relax. Nevertheless, life with Colin, particularly in the early years, almost destroyed me. I had to learn how to cope, how to get around Colin and, slowly, how to make sure I didn't disappear under the strain.

Today I would not recommend someone to stay in a marriage like mine, but I have no regrets about the choices I made. I did what I thought was right, Colin didn't break my spirit, and it has led me to the life I'm enjoying so much now. Nonetheless I'm glad so much has changed. Marriage is no longer compulsory, and people now have the chance to make an informed choice about the person they will share their lives with, which I did not. Crucially, men and women are now brought up, I hope and believe, to think of themselves as equals, even if the care of children is still regarded as primarily the responsibility of the mother. Gay marriage has meant that there are lots of different types of committed partnerships today. All around me in Norfolk there are married couples of all kinds, and it's splendid that so many can now enjoy the security and commitment of the marriage bond if they so desire.

It was very different in my day and there was no doubt what being a wife meant for women like me. A wife had to be a credit and ornament to their husbands, have children, and run their husband's households. Given these expectations, no wonder some husbands treated their wives as servants or chattels. We were also expected to choose a spouse and make our vows on the basis of very short acquaintance. Sex before marriage was unthinkable for a girl from my background, and divorce a shameful admission of failure. Growing up, I accepted these beliefs, but I had no idea what they might lead to in practice.

I rather enjoy having to explain in talks what 'coming out' meant in the fifties – it was official recognition we were ready for marriage. Certainly not what it means now! Once we were launched on society, we were expected to marry quickly and make what our friends and family would regard as a good match. I was delighted that this new stage of my life was beginning, and once I got over my nerves, I did enjoy all the parties and dances. The idea of going to university or having a career simply didn't occur to me. I was looking forward to having a husband, a large family, and a marriage that looked very much like that of my parents.

Like most young women I was terribly romantic. I wanted to marry for love and feel that passionate spark for the person I was going to share my life with. I met Colin in the bar at the Ritz at a debutante dance a year or so after I was maid of honour at the Queen's Coronation, and I liked him very much. He was so different from all my father's dull choices of the shooting fraternity. He was very good-looking, charming, a marvellous dancer and, best of all, he could talk about more than shooting and fishing. He loved art and design and was extremely knowledgeable about both subjects, but he didn't deliver long lectures. He always talked with infectious enthusiasm about everything he was interested in. He was a brilliant storyteller and gloried in gossip and laughter. He was also part of Princess Margaret's set, and knew all sorts of glamorous people, writers and artists. He seemed like a glorious breath of fresh air. I fell in love with him and was delighted when he proposed.

When I saw something of Colin's anger while we were engaged, I was young and naive enough to believe him when he told me that after we were married he would be so happy he would never have to lose his temper again. I am certain no one ever mentioned to me that he had suffered two nervous breakdowns before we met, one severe enough for him to have spent time in a clinic in Switzerland. When we married in April 1956, I had known him for less than a year.

I was also totally ignorant about sex. I'd never slept with anyone before marrying Colin or spent much time alone with him. The risks of unwanted pregnancy were too high for us to break the strict code. If I'd hoped that Colin would help me learn about sex with gentleness and kindness, I was wrong. Colin had a tantrum that left him exhausted on our wedding night in Paris, so that was a non-starter, and the actual consummation, when it happened, was awkward, painful and not particularly enjoyable or romantic. Apparently this was my fault.

When he took me to a brothel a night or two later to watch a private sex show I felt he was saying, 'You're hopeless at it but you'll get some good tips from watching this.' It was so humiliating. I assumed he was experienced when we married, which he was, having had numerous affairs before we met, but that did not mean he regarded it as his role to teach me how to explore this side of life with gentleness or generosity. As long as Colin and I were sleeping together, our sex life was marked by criticism and disappointment. He used to get very cross with me, which of course made things worse and I used to dread going to bed with him. I tried to be enthusiastic, but it never worked between us and for a very long time I felt I must be to blame for that.

The one time he seemed pleased with me was years later in the Grenadines. I think he arranged for my drink to be spiked and, from what I know now, I suspect it was LSD. I had the most terrifying experience, with visions and hallucinations, but we ended up making passionate love despite my feeling so scared. It was extremely energetic and uninhibited.

The next day, Colin said, 'That was amazing, and that's the way I want you to behave all the time.'

'Well, I felt awful and I still do,' I replied.

He didn't lace my drink again, but how strange and somehow typical of Colin that, rather than being tender, he decided he could just drug me into doing what he liked.

Our honeymoon was supposed to last six months, but to my great relief we came back after three. I had become pregnant almost immediately and had terrible morning sickness, which meant we had to return home. Given that our whole purpose as women was to marry and produce children, one might have thought this meant the honeymoon had been a success, but I came back in shock. I went to my mother in a panic to tell her that I didn't think I could carry on with Colin and his terrible tantrums. She told me I'd made my choice and should stick with it. No complaining was allowed, to our husbands or to anyone else, so when I appealed to her I got very short shrift. She made it clear she expected me to cope and keep my troubles to myself, so that was what I tried to do.

I was following the example she had set. My father could be very difficult but my mother made it clear that we must adapt to him, make endless allowances, and never rebuke him. She was preparing me for a lifetime of mollifying difficult men. I don't blame her. When, many years later the worst happened, I had her support, but she was bringing me up to cope with a fundamental truth of my class and time: women must put up and shut up.

Just about every other woman I knew was told they had to soldier on and not complain. Even the Queen, the head of state, worked hard to make sure her husband was kept happy. My role as Colin's wife was all about doing what he wanted, sorting out his messes and appearing cheerful while I did it. That much had been made very clear to me.

Another side of Colin that would test me was his constant restlessness. When we returned from our honeymoon early we had nowhere to live so stayed with his mother, Pamela, in her commodious house in Notting Hill. That only increased the stunned shock I'd been feeling since the very first day of our marriage. When I tried to turn to Pamela for advice on how to handle Colin's outbursts, she said to me that the best thing to do was to give him a nice cup of cocoa at bedtime! There clearly wasn't going to be much help from that quarter.

Like Colin, Pamela was charming but rather spoiled and childish, so life with both of them while I was suffering from morning sickness was far from easy. We soon moved out, but into a tiny flat. Its linoleum floor smelt awful, which added to my nausea and misery. Thank goodness our friend Patrick Plunket came to the rescue, offering us his brother's house in Kent on a long let while he was away. Now we had more room, fresh air, and a routine, with Colin going off to work in the City every day. We had to give up that house when the lease ended.

After Charlie was born, Colin announced that he'd bought a mews house in Knightsbridge. I was startled as

I hadn't even seen it, and when I did, I was disappointed. It was a grand address, but the house was dark, cramped and rather oppressive.

It was already becoming clear that I would have to get used to moving frequently. Nothing ever satisfied Colin for long. Each new house was a blank canvas for him to try out his skills as a decorator, an opportunity he relished. He was very talented and knowledgeable about everything to do with design and architecture, and he taught me so much as he went along. The downside was that he was so adamant about what he did and didn't like that he couldn't be happy unless everything was perfect.

I was, of course, expected to follow wherever he went, and was rarely consulted on where that might be. Even when we seemed to be settled in one place, I might be told that the house had been sold from under us and there was a week or at most a fortnight to pack the entire contents and leave. Sometimes, if Colin was away or too busy doing other things, I had to find another house for us all to live in during that time as well. It was a giddy, challenging experience. The only permanence for me was the few possessions I took with me to each new home, my little things – photographs, favourite chairs and pictures. I found them a great comfort, and I was always able to find a private spot for the belongings I cared for most. I learned how to carve my own small sanctuary out of the chaos.

I was so happy when my father, seeing me go through the turmoil of moving so often, persuaded me to buy my own home on the Holkham estate. My farmhouse there was mine. Colin had no say over the decoration so I could do what I wanted. I gradually filled it with my books, paintings and photographs and it became a stable point for me and the children. Colin disliked it and hardly ever came, which also turned out to be a great relief. It is still my home today: I'm writing this book in my sunny sitting room, surrounded by small treasures I've collected over the years, all of which remind me of some special occasion or friend, and looking out over the garden I have tended for fifty years. It's been a wonderful refuge ever since.

While I was pregnant, I realised that Colin was never going to help me with my anxieties and problems and I would have to find a way to cope on my own. Although really our only purpose as women was to marry and have children, young brides like myself were told very little about how that would all come about, or how to cope with it. It seems absurd how in the dark we were about the facts of life and what pregnancy and childbirth would be like, let alone early motherhood. It's unthinkable now not to educate young women about these things.

I have never known anything like the sickness I endured when I was pregnant with Charlie. Colin's behaviour did not make things any easier. In the early days, I had almost no sleep as night after night, Colin lay in a foetal position on the floor, or sat rocking back and forth, wailing non-stop for hours about how awful his life was, and how it was everybody's fault but his. He would complain endlessly to me, waking me up to pour out his woes about how he'd been treated as a child, his parents' divorce and the fact he wasn't given more responsibility by his father in the family company. I listened patiently and sympathetically, but it didn't seem to do any good. I made no difference to his state of mind and became exhausted.

I felt utterly wretched and I was in such agonising pain that they took out my appendix when I was six months pregnant. Of course it didn't help as there was nothing wrong with my appendix. After Colin died, I was shocked to discover something he had written to the effect that I'd had the operation on purpose, which might have endangered Charlie's life. It was perhaps the most hurtful thing he ever said, and I'm glad he was no longer alive when I read it. I couldn't think why he would ever believe such an appalling thing. I wanted very much to be a mother, but there was no doubt I suffered a great deal. I now think all that pain was a symptom of the shock and strain of finding myself married to someone like Colin and the effort involved in coping with it all.

Women did have some preparation for the happy event. Before we gave birth, expectant mothers went off to see a lady who made us lie on the floor, pant and breathe, pant and breathe. It all seemed very easy. Obviously childbirth was going to be a breeze once you got the breathing right. But when it was happening and the pain had begun, I forgot all I had been taught and shouted for the gas and air! This was all we had for pain relief. I like the idea of an epidural. I imagine being able to sit and read a book, perhaps eat a grape or two, while one's body does all the hard work. Gas and air was worse than useless: it just made me terribly thirsty. Colin was with me for a while but he was so agitated that eventually the doctor said, 'Could you please get rid of your husband?' My mother took him out for dinner.

Childbirth *was* jolly, jolly painful, and when Charlie arrived safely, it was a huge relief. We were all delighted that we had a beautiful healthy son and heir. But I was rather shell-shocked by the experience, to say the least.

Just before Charlie was born, my mother said she'd give me a cot so, like everyone else I knew, I went into Harrods to choose one. I was quite overwhelmed: the cots were wonderful. They had huge flounces, lace, organza and marvellous embroidered cushions. The one I chose was amazing, trimmed with red ribbons and made up with fine linen sheets. It really was a work of art. After making that choice, it seemed all further decisions about how to look after the baby were to be made by Nanny.

Looking back, I now wish I'd been able to assert myself a little more after Charlie's birth, but I was still in shock. In short order, I'd married Colin, had a traumatic honeymoon, moved house three times, and begun to realise what

I'd got myself into. I wonder if the strain and anxiety this produced helped to make Charlie such a difficult baby. He was fretful and never seemed to need to sleep at all. While my friends' babies took naps and slept for at least a few hours at a time, giving some blessed peace, Charlie seemed always to be awake. I don't know how he managed it.

I was walking on eggshells to guard against Colin's temper but I was also at the mercy of Nanny. Our first nanny was called Nanny White, and she moved into the second bedroom in our house, while Charlie was in the box room. Nanny White adored Charlie to the extent that I wasn't really allowed to have much to do with him. I longed to have more time with him, but Nanny made it very hard. From the start she was very possessive and kept me at arm's length.

The few times I looked after him at night he would start howling, and I'd be terribly nervous that he'd wake Colin, who was irate if his sleep was disturbed. I'd spend ages hushing the baby, keeping an ear out for Colin. It was exhausting. Some nights I really did feel at the end of my tether, in a state of panic that I couldn't possibly show or I'd make everything worse. I tried everything I could, even bringing Charlie into our bed, but that only made Colin cross. Then I'd walk around the house all night, feeling desperately stressed. It's no wonder Charlie was an anxious, moody child considering how I was feeling most of the time.

Nanny White wasn't easy but Charlie adored her. I got pregnant again, and had a much better time of it. Just after I'd had Henry I was up in Norfolk with my monthly nurse, leaving Nanny White at our country house with Charlie. Colin suddenly sacked her.

Charlie, only three years old, was devastated and naturally thought it was Henry's fault that his beloved nanny had disappeared. He ran off into a cornfield and couldn't be found for ages. I really believe now the poor little boy had something like a nervous breakdown.

'Why on earth did you sack her like that?' I asked.

'She was very annoying,' Colin said. 'And I thought you didn't like her. I did it for you.'

'She was difficult,' I said, 'but surely you must realise that this is the worst possible thing we could do for Charlie.'

I was exasperated because I was certain that if I'd been there I could have smoothed things over and made it all right but it was too late. I think it made poor Charlie's problems worse and he didn't really like his baby brother for a long time after that. A succession of nannies followed, and the care of both boys was largely left to them. Like my mother, I saw my children only at certain times of day, for an hour or so in the morning or evening.

The rule was husband first, children second, which in our case meant that Colin and I were often away for weekends and had endless engagements during the week. Then in 1958 Colin bought Mustique and, of course, I was expected to spend weeks at a time with him in the West Indies as we explored the island. It's no surprise that Charlie and Henry felt that Colin and I were distant parents.

By the time Henry arrived, we were on our fifth move, to Old Park Farm in Essex, where I finally had a bedroom big enough for my own four-poster bed. It was my longed-for private space. Separate bedrooms and bathrooms helped me a great deal. I found it easier to play the role of Colin's wife to an acceptable standard when I had a space of my own to retreat to, however briefly.

By now I had begun to feel as though I was a non-person, only good for sorting out Colin's problems but not worth anything myself. Not only was Colin's temper on a hair trigger at all times, but I was astonished to find myself blamed for everything that went wrong, or everything that he felt had gone wrong. I had to learn very quickly how to deal with his sudden demands, defuse difficult situations and move swiftly to repair any damage his behaviour had caused. Everything irritated him. The trigger for an almighty meltdown could come from the most unpredictable place. He would lose his temper in an instant and give you very little time to put right whatever he'd objected to. I learned to stay calm, be vigilant, and weather the storms. Of course I had a great deal of help at home, with nannies and cooks and maids, but I still had to bear the brunt of his temper and take the blame for his misery.

From the earliest days of our marriage, everything went one way: from me to Colin. His own feelings took precedence in any and every situation. How exhausting and how lonely it could be. I felt as though parts of me were dying, with no one to nurture or cherish me when I needed it. It was like having another child, but a particularly large and disruptive one. He shocked, offended and, frankly, terrified other people most of the time, and I had to sort out the results. Too often I existed just as a buffer between him and everyone else.

Yet still, in the midst of it all, there were moments of vivid happiness – and dancing was one of them. In our early marriage we often went to jazz clubs in Soho or other clubs where we could let rip on the dance-floor. I remember one place where we went upstairs in a lift and, hearing the music before we reached the top, were dancing together before the doors had even opened. We loved jive and rock and roll. To me, Colin was at his most attractive on the dance-floor, and those were really magical times. I could forget myself, and all the tensions between us, and I learned to grasp every pleasure I could. I'm sure those moments helped me take the continual dramas in my stride.

Colin's restlessness meant a lot of travelling. I went with him on many occasions, too many to count, but one of the hazards of travelling with him was that I always had to carry his luggage as he claimed he wasn't strong enough. I was like a packhorse, always labouring behind him, laden with cases. It was often frightfully embarrassing in airports as there would be a huge queue of people waiting to check in, and Colin would simply march to the front, while I followed, strung with luggage.

'Come on, Anne,' he'd order loudly. 'Put my cases on that conveyor.'

The amazing thing was that, apart from a few grumbles, people didn't complain. They seemed so amazed at his effrontery that they just let it happen and didn't protest, not that Colin would have taken any notice if they had. Once, on holiday with my friend Nicky, I automatically picked up his case and started carrying it. He said, 'Why on earth are you doing that?'

And I said, 'I'm just too used to it. I couldn't help it!'

Many people have proffered a diagnosis of Colin. I have no idea why he behaved as he did, though I can make some guesses.

After Colin's brother was born, his mother, Pamela, took to her bed and refused to leave her room. He used to hear his father screaming at her through the closed door. They parted when Colin was about nine and he had little contact with his father after that, though he got on very well with his stepmother, Elizabeth. She was one of the few people he chose to behave well around. Colin used to complain that his father's secretary would choose his Christmas and birthday presents and his father wouldn't even sign his cards himself, leaving that to the secretary too. His father certainly wasn't affectionate, and Colin was confused when Charlie and Henry tried to hug or kiss him when they were little. Like me, Colin was raised by a series of nannies, but as a boy he went away to school much earlier than I did, and he didn't have someone in his life like my mother, or a nurturing presence like Billy Williams. I grew very fond of Pamela, but she could be difficult and selfish too. She and Colin's father were prone to dreadful rages.

Colin was a clever, good-looking little boy, so he was also indulged by the people looking after him. Later in life, when he realised he couldn't charm everyone into doing whatever he wanted immediately, he responded with terrible rages.

Something was always pushing Colin on – his desire to acquire things was a huge force in his later life. He would dash around sale rooms, creating impressive collections, and would sell them without regret.

Colin was so frightfully impatient. It all had to happen *now, now, now*! He was always rushing and shouting, 'Keep up! Keep up!' That led to some great expeditions, but was obviously a terrible strain.

Perhaps he lacked a filter that most other people have. He certainly didn't receive the kind of training I'd had to put the needs of others first. Quite the opposite. His needs were always the priority.

Ten years into my marriage, I took a lover, which did me an enormous amount of good. Husbands, who usually held all the financial cards, were often flagrantly unfaithful.

Colin was, from the earliest days of our marriage. For the most part, wives simply put up with it and didn't make a fuss, but many made arrangements of their own. I am so glad I had that opportunity. I had been taught to think of divorce as impossible, but I was in great need of some kindness and cherishing, and enjoying some of that affection changed my life. Our relationship lasted for thirty-four years, until my friend died. I was very lucky. It was perfect, even though it was only lunch once a week and the occasional magical weekend when we were able escape together. It was difficult to arrange but we managed it. It was only with my friend that I realised how amazing sex could be, and what I had been missing. While I was so grateful to experience that, I couldn't help feeling sad that it had been so difficult with Colin. It's hard not to feel cross now. I finally discovered it takes two to have great sex, so it was always going to be difficult with someone who only considered his own wants. I no longer had to blame myself for those difficulties. A good love life is one of life's gifts and a great bond for any couple.

My friend's wife was very generous to me. She knew about our arrangement and, in fact, had one of her own. There was no question of any of us leaving our marriages, though. It simply wasn't done and I don't think we ever considered it. When my friend was dying, his wife rang me up and said he would like to say goodbye to me, so I was able to see him in his last days. I was always grateful to her for that, and that she sent me a memento of him after he died.

Colin, however, wasn't pleased. He was terribly jealous. One of the things that annoyed him was that my friend wasn't particularly good-looking and Colin couldn't understand it: he was so good-looking and perfect, how on earth could I want to be with anyone else? The fact I might enjoy the company, in and out of bed, of someone who was consistently kind to me, didn't seem to occur to him.

There wasn't much Colin could do about my friendship, considering he was unfaithful all the time and didn't bother hiding it. There was one long-term mistress who was particularly painful for me. He didn't tell me about her, but I saw them together at a party and knew at once just by the way they were standing together that they were intimate. I said nothing but eventually Colin told me himself. This mistress tried very hard to make him marry her, but he never left me. As long as I could tolerate his extramarital affairs without tears and tantrums, and remain discreet, he would stay with me. And of course he could hardly complain when the boot was on the other foot so he put up with it. But he didn't like it.

After a gap of eight years, and some problems conceiving I discovered I was pregnant again, and our third son, Christopher, was born in 1968. His birth heralded the arrival of Barbara Barnes in our lives, as our new nanny. She came from Holkham and had even sung in the choir at my wedding. Christopher adored her. In the coming years she completely transformed my life, helped me become a great deal more confident as a mother and succeed in finding my separate space away from Colin. She remained with us until 1982 when she left to become nanny to Princes William and Harry and remains a friend to this day. This was also the year we moved into the White House in Tite Street, which was to be our home for more than a decade. It marked the happiest period of our marriage.

Colin had actually bought the White House in 1963. It had been built by the artist James Whistler in 1877 and was completely run down and shifting towards the Thames, as it had no foundations. Colin had been planning to restore it but, realising it was past saving, he decided to completely demolish it and have it rebuilt to a new, modern design. It took five years, a lot of fights over planning permissions, and the finished result was divisive, but I thought it was unquestionably a great achievement, the inside matching the outside for beauty, every detail planned by Colin. The decoration was lavish, with marble, silk, silver and fine Portland stone, and audacious, with some amazing decorative plastic windows that looked like stained glass and sent wonderful coloured shadows all around the hall. Colin helped to design the patterned marble floors, the graceful cantilevered staircase and even the shell-shaped door furniture. I really believe it was his masterpiece, and once we moved in, living there was a very special experience. For once Colin was also happy with what he'd achieved.

I now had a really rather grand set of my own rooms, which not only offered me substantial space away from Colin, but which were quite amazing. I was allowed to choose my own bedroom decoration and had a beautiful floral chintz designed especially for me, and made into curtains. My precious four-poster bed was now hung in pink pleated silk. A specially woven Aubusson carpet of scattered daisies covered the floor. It was all perfect. The pleasure of that bedroom, and the view it offered of the Thames from my window, still lives with me. My bathroom was decorated in bespoke tiles in an eighteenth-century design with great cornucopias of fruit and flowers. These were Colin's idea too and I loved them, and hugely enjoyed going to Holland with him to visit the tile museum, select the design to be copied, and see where the tiles would be made. How strange it seems now to say I was 'allowed' to choose my own decoration, but at that time and in my marriage it was presented as a gracious concession on Colin's part, and I accepted it as such. I liked it much better than any of the dank shooting lodges my other suitors might have offered to me as a home.

I did try to make my opinion known about other areas of the house, but it never counted for much. Colin didn't really see the point of kitchens, as he didn't eat much or cook anything, or see the need for storage: places to put the brooms, buckets and Hoovers, hang coats or keep toys. He couldn't bear it if they might spoil the design or ruin the symmetry.

He was completely impractical and designed houses more as though they were stage sets than places to live, which was why he got on so well with Oliver Messel, who designed the houses on Mustique, and who was primarily a stage and set designer. Practical spaces bored him.

'Kitchens are frightfully common, Anne,' he would say. 'Why do you have to keep banging on about them? A kettle and a toaster are all you need.'

Eventually our architect talked him into having quite a decent kitchen, interesting him in it as somewhere he could show off his advanced design skills and love of modern appliances. On that basis, he could accept the idea of a kitchen.

It took me a long time to learn that a wife didn't have to be subservient, and to see that the best marriages were those of equals, with each partner looking after the other, instead of one doing all the ministering. Nowadays I always feel nervous around marriages where I sense one party in control. My antennae for that are highly developed and I can often feel when the power is disproportionately weighted to one side. I don't think it's really ever healthy.

There were some successful marriages in my generation. My good friends Zanna and Nicky Johnston had an unconventional but very successful marriage, but the best I ever saw was that of my cousin David Airlie. He and his wife Ginny have always been a team, completely equal, genuinely happy in one another's company and living in amicable friendship with shared interests. Thinking of that relationship, I can't help feeling a little wistful for what life might have been like with a strong, secure marriage of equals, each looking out for the other, and living a life of mutual respect, love and kindness.

In general, however, even when a marriage among my contemporaries started with love and affection, it was often impossible to maintain for long given the unequal way in which men and women were brought up: women were there to serve men, a powerful message, and once the first rush of romantic love wore off, men often felt their part of the bargain was now complete.

The very worst of all was when cruelty was coupled with a charmless, boorish personality. My poor sister Carey experienced this, with a husband who would only talk to her through the dog for years on end. Her life was miserable tedium and my mother and I encouraged her to leave him, but she never did. She got to the point of arranging somewhere else to live but on the brink of going she was persuaded to stay. They descended into alcoholism and it was very sad. And such a waste. As much as I think that divorce should be avoided if at all possible, in some cases it is the best outcome.

So, I shan't pretend my life was like Carey's, with a husband ordering the Labrador to 'tell that awful woman the fire needs some logs'. My life had parties, people, travel, with lots of remarkable friends.

Around the time we moved into Tite Street I learned that talking about my problems as opposed to ignoring them could be of enormous benefit. Colin liked to be ahead of the curve and went to therapy – 'to see my shrink', as he put it, feeling very fashionable, no doubt – but it seemed to make very little difference to his mental wellbeing. Then he told me that he lay in complete silence for the entire session.

'Don't you say anything?' I asked disbelievingly. This therapist was not cheap and came highly recommended.

'Not a word,' Colin said, as though this was a major personal triumph. I think he was pleased with himself for managing to come up with a new take on talking therapy: saying absolutely nothing. That must have been hard, given how difficult he found it to stay still.

These silent sessions didn't help him in any way I noticed, any more than pouring out his troubles to me had done, but for a while sitting in furious silence with his shrink meant the need to tell me all his troubles was lessened. When his therapist died suddenly it just added to the trauma and I resumed my role as recipient of Colin's woes. My own stress levels rose accordingly. Desperate, I went to our family doctor telling him I really needed help, and he referred me to my own therapist. He persuaded me that it would not only benefit me but help me learn to cope with Colin.

At the very first session with my therapist, I was apprehensive and unsure of where to start. I lay down to talk and, to my surprise, instead of talking about Colin as I fully expected to, I started by recounting my experience with Miss Bonner all those years before, her cruelty and how, no matter what I did, I was punished every night. As I talked, I realised that I was completely paralysed. It was terrifying, I really couldn't move a muscle. In a complete panic, I stammered out that I couldn't move. The therapist calmed me and told me that if I relaxed, it would pass, which fortunately it did.

It was a very strange experience, but it made me understand the depths of the old wounds that I needed to explore and come to terms with. Only when I wrote my novel *A Haunting at Holkham* many years later did I finally let go of what had happened. Reliving the experience in fiction, I finally found I could be in control and didn't need to be a frightened child any more.

I ended up talking a great deal with my therapist about Colin, too, and it helped enormously. Although I didn't develop any tools to help him, I realised, crucially, that he couldn't *be* helped. There was nothing I could solve for him. Whatever had happened to Colin to make him the way he was had happened in his childhood and I could never change him, and, unless he could put in the work, he would certainly never change himself. I began to have a little more sympathy for him – and it helped me to absolve myself of responsibility for him too. Very importantly, it gave me the strength to believe in my worth as my own person.

I began to see clearly how tired I was. Colin was so very exhausting to live with. There was no room for me as a person because I was always so busy looking after him and anticipating his needs as well as protecting the children. Of course I wasn't used to any other life so I didn't miss it or expect anything else from being married. I was just sorry I wasn't as good at managing as my mother had been, and believed that some of those tantrums were my fault. Therapy helped me to see that I needed to stop trying to be the 'good wife' at such a great cost to my own mental wellbeing. However many of Colin's storms and tantrums I prevented or smoothed over, there would always be something that drove him into a frenzy. I had to start to find something for myself in life.

Sometimes I find that talking too much about life's problems can simply make one more agitated and prolong the misery. Friends mean well, but they tend to sympathise and tell you you're right to be so upset and egg you on to feel wronged. That can actually make things worse if you let it. Therapy is very different. You have one hour, and someone who listens calmly and offers advice from a more distanced perspective. I do recommend it for anyone who has the opportunity to try it. I learned a great deal about myself, and about Colin, and it was one of the things that gave me the strength and resilience to cope.

I went to therapy for perhaps a year, but stopped shortly before the twins, Amy and May, were born in 1970 as I really couldn't see how I would manage it with two new babies. Princess Margaret offered me a lifeline at around the same time when she asked me to be her lady in waiting. She could see that I needed a form of escape from Colin and my royal duties were not something he would protest against. In fact, Colin was thrilled as he thought it meant he could come, too, when we travelled abroad. I told him it was not going to be like that. But he was proud of my position close to Princess Margaret, just as he liked my aristocratic background despite cultivating an air of being terribly unconventional. Another paradox. Having a chance to take a break from Colin's demands and problems meant it was a great deal easier to appreciate the advantages of being his wife when we were together, the friends, the whirling adventure of it all, the laughter and companionship. I also found that dealing with Colin for years had turned me into something of a diplomat. I was gradually growing more resilient, developing more faith in myself and my abilities, more confident as a mother, and through my role as a lady in waiting, spending more time supporting charitable causes.

Perhaps it is telling that it was around this time I became involved with Erin Pizzey's pioneering work: she established the first domestic-violence shelter in the UK in 1971, then known as the Chiswick Women's Shelter. It grew rapidly to become Refuge, the largest charity in the world providing help for victims of this often hidden and awful abuse. I felt privileged to be able to help with fundraising and visited the shelters frequently. This may seem very odd now, but even after that time in therapy, it never occurred to me that this interest might be founded on my own experiences with Colin. I think now that Erin Pizzey perhaps saw something in me that told her I should get involved, or would be sympathetic to the cause.

I wrote about Colin's rages and tantrums in *Lady in Waiting*, but I wrote about them in the same way I usually talked about those incidents with my friends, even my closest friends, lightheartedly, emphasising what was funny or ridiculous, and laughing at his behaviour rather than admitting frankly the deep humiliation and distress it often caused. Sometimes we'd try to work out why he behaved as he did, but more often than not we'd simply laugh. Laughing – even at the blackest of memories – can make things much better. I'll always look for the humour, the absurd in even the darkest corner to make everything more bearable. It is a great release and has helped me enormously.

I also took my courage from Princess Margaret, who was a great believer that one didn't dwell. When her husband

Tony, Earl of Snowdon, was being unfaithful to her, and there were lots of sadnesses and awful things to endure in his behaviour, we would talk about it but not at great length. Then we would concentrate on other things that we knew would make us feel better. I saw Princess Margaret putting up with all manner of things that could have upset her very much. She simply concentrated on getting through it knowing that afterwards it would never seem as important or terrible as it had at the time.

This resolution struck me as a form of courage. She hated crying. Once when I didn't open a door quickly enough for Colin, and he blew up and she saw me start to cry, she just said, 'Stop that at once, Anne. It's absolutely no use.'

And she was right.

I learned a lot about stiffening one's spine and getting on with it from Princess Margaret and I'm very grateful to her for that.

For years I coped with ignoring or suppressing my feelings, and when I struggled to put a brave face on Colin's behaviour, I learned ways of giving myself time to recover, and getting away from him by sailing or reading in a gypsy caravan I kept on the grounds of Glen, our house in Scotland. Those retreats gave me a chance to get the noise of his constant complaints and demands out of my ears. I found they gave me the strength to carry on and face whatever storms came next. I also learned to treasure the many moments of joy and laughter we shared with our family and friends, and appreciate the times Colin was at his best, charming and enthusing the people around us. That was until a great change came in our marriage. It would test me to my very limit.

Buying Mustique was a great leap into the unknown, and I had some marvellous times on the island, even in the early days when we had no running water or electricity. It was wonderful to see it develop and spend time there with friends, including Princess Margaret, who was with us often from the early days.

Spending so much time out in the West Indies, however, was not good for Colin. His arrival had improved the lives of the islanders a great deal in material terms. He built a new village, brought electricity to the island and created a lot of well-paying jobs by attracting so many wealthy new landowners. Over the years he also sank a lot of his personal fortune into the island. As a result, he regarded himself as the King of Mustique and behaved accordingly, as a monarch with absolute power, and in his rages he would attack people physically. I'm afraid that many of the islanders simply accepted this as what white men did. Colin would often be very generous, paying for medical treatment, setting people up in business or funding the education of the children who lived on Mustique, so they accepted his awful behaviour as the price to be paid for the advantages he brought. He got used to being able to indulge his worst rages without facing any consequences whatsoever. It was not just the islanders who indulged him: even the wealthy men and women with homes on the island simply ignored his behaviour – a battle with the King of Mustique simply wasn't worth having.

Perhaps I shouldn't be surprised then that when he finally did attack me it was on the island. It was November in the late seventies and we were celebrating the twins' birthday. We had gone down to Basil's Bar to celebrate over a high tea with Barbara, the girls' nanny, and a few friends. Colin was in the bar having drinks with clients, while I sat with the children. After a while, he came over and asked me to go and meet the people he was talking to and have a drink, no doubt to soften them up for his business deal.

I didn't really want to, but I left the children with Barbara and went over. I was introduced, said a nice hello and chatted for a few minutes, then explained politely about the birthday party and went back to the twins. A little while later Colin marched over, white with fury. Through clenched teeth he commanded, 'Come with me.'

Before I could say anything, he grabbed my arm and pulled me out of the bar with him. I knew I was in trouble but, not wanting to make a fuss, I did not resist and went with him.

I asked my daughter May recently if she remembered that day, and she did. 'I told Barbara I thought Daddy was going to be cruel to you, but she told me not to worry.'

On the way back to our house in the car, a journey of about ten minutes, Colin was silent, but shaking with anger. I also stayed very still and quiet, my usual tactic from the earliest days of our marriage when he was in a rage, hoping he would calm down.

We drew up at the house, I got out of the car and before I knew what was happening he hit me across the head from behind with his shark-bone walking stick. It knocked me straight to the ground, and then he launched in on me. I lay there, trying to protect my head and begging him to stop. He didn't: he was in a frenzy, quite out of his mind. I was utterly terrified, convinced he might actually kill me.

I have no idea how long it lasted, but eventually he tired himself out. I lay there without moving until I heard his car drive off, then crawled into the main house where my bedroom was and locked the door. I was petrified he might come back in the same state and finish me off.

Later I learned that Colin went back to the bar and told a friend of ours without a trace of remorse, 'I've just given Anne a thrashing.' And the friend did nothing. He didn't go to Barbara or fetch any help or come and check on me. I honestly don't know why he didn't. Perhaps he had that old idea of not wanting to interfere between husband and wife. Perhaps he thought it wasn't his place – but, then, whose place was it? Perhaps he didn't want to risk the embarrassment of incurring Colin's wrath himself, but I would have thought he could still have told Barbara I might need some help. Or perhaps he thought Colin was exaggerating. I try not to dwell on it even now, but the idea of Colin going back to the bar and actually boasting about what he had just done is truly horrible.

I was alone all night and in agony. By the next morning, I realised something was seriously wrong and I needed a doctor. The pain in my ear was terrible. I knew I was covered with blood as I could feel it matted into my hair but I didn't dare look at myself and I was too scared to come out of the bedroom through the door in case Colin was waiting outside. I was certain that he had gone completely mad. I crawled out of the window as dawn was breaking and reached Barbara's chalet nearby in the grounds. I will never forget the look of shock and horror on her face when she saw me.

Barbara took me back to my room, phoned the doctor and then told Colin exactly what she thought of him. I heard her give him absolute hell through the closed door. 'How dare you?' she shouted. 'How dare you treat Lady Anne like that? It's unforgivable!'

It was very brave of her, but then she had always been able to deal with Colin when he was at his worst while I never could. Colin slunk off, and the island's doctor arrived and examined me. He was very concerned but I didn't tell him what had happened and he didn't ask. Perhaps he guessed. My eardrum was burst, and I have been deaf in that ear ever since.

For perhaps the first time in his life, Colin knew he had gone too far. He wanted to see me but Barbara forbade it. Instead he left a small bunch of flowers outside my room. I didn't want the flowers.

My injuries meant I couldn't fly for some time. For the next few days I kept to my room. I did not want the children to see me until the bruises had healed. Barbara looked after me. Goodness knows what she told the children – probably that I wasn't feeling well and needed rest. They were used to her so I don't think they were particularly worried about me.

Once I was able to emerge, Colin was allowed to see me, and he said a meek sorry, like a little boy. 'I won't do it again,' he said. 'I will be good, I promise.'

It was one of the only times I saw any real remorse from him about his behaviour.

I said nothing. He was sorry he was in trouble, and that he'd gone too far. That was all.

I stayed in the house and away from the children for about ten days until my bruises had faded. The day before I was able to fly back, I went down to the beach and one of the better-known people on the island, a woman I'd known for some time and counted as a friend, came up to me in the bar. She looked at my face and arms, where bruises were still visible, despite the makeup I'd put on to cover them.

'Have you been a naughty girl?' she asked.

'Of course not,' I said, but couldn't say anything else.

It was so painful and humiliating. Did she expect me to joke about it? I'm afraid I really hated her in that moment.

On my return to England, I told my mother everything. I felt she had to know how far Colin was willing to go in his treatment of me. Years ago she had told me I'd made my bed and had to lie in it. Did she still think that now, once she knew what he had become capable of? He could easily have killed me.

She was horrified. She had grown to like Colin even though she'd always known something of what I put up with, but now she asked if I wanted to leave him.

In different circumstances, Colin could have been arrested for what he had done to me. Many would say he should have been, and for the casual assaults he perpetrated against others. It seems incredible now what we allowed him to get away with. Of course many people on the island worked for him, so were in a difficult position, and perhaps they, like me, just accepted his behaviour as inevitable, something that had to be endured. I could have gone to the police in England, but I was too ashamed to make public what had happened and too loyal to the family to bring the inevitable press interest and prurient tittle-tattle. I also still believed in marriage, and in the virtue of putting up with things and getting on.

I had noticed when I worked with Erin Pizzey that the wives often blamed themselves for their husbands' behaviour, and I'm afraid even on this occasion I began to think I was partly to blame. After all, I knew how volatile he was, so perhaps I should have avoided making him angry, however much I wanted to enjoy the girls' birthday party with them. It was an attempt, I suppose, to rationalise the whole thing, as if I could make it better by blaming myself to some extent.

Colin and I had been married for more than twenty years and he was a fundamental part of my life. Something in me had irrevocably changed towards him, but I still felt that I couldn't take that final step and divorce him. When I told my mother my decision, she got hold of Colin and issued our ultimatum. 'If you ever do anything like that to Anne again, that's it. She'll leave and we will support her in every way.'

Colin grovelled. I believe he was ashamed of what he'd done once the people he respected confronted him with it, and with the consequences. He also wrote me a proper apology, saying in effect *I can see why you'd leave me, but please don't because I will be good from now on.* I don't think people understand how hard it can be to leave someone who can be so awful at some moments, then so sad and sorry at others.

Despite my accepting his apology, things were never the same between us. That extraordinary and unprovoked rage had shown me a sadistic streak and a depth of cruelty I could never forget. Colin never hit me again, although he did still push me and spit at me when furious. He knew enough never to go further than that.

I eventually found a kind of acceptance that enabled me to move on. I didn't accept that I should go on suffering, or be treated in that way again, but I accepted that it had happened, and what it told me about Colin. He was my husband, but I had to keep my distance and protect myself. No matter how badly he treated me, he needed me. He used to threaten to kill himself if I left him, and I didn't see that as an idle threat. I knew I was important to him as a point of stability in his life, and as mother to his children. In his own strange way, he loved me and needed me. I made my peace with the situation. I could go on being married, and go on loving Colin and caring for him as much as I could, but I had to take care of myself too.

This became easier once I stopped blaming myself for his outbursts, and we spent more and more time apart. We had already moved out of the White House to Hill Lodge, because Colin needed money for Mustique, and when Hill Lodge was also sold I bought my London flat. Though we still spent a lot of time together, we no longer shared a permanent home. I looked after him as much as I could. I was still his wife and that meant helping to plan and then being at his side in public at his extravagant parties on Mustique and caring for him in private when it was possible. We still made each other laugh and spent many happy times together with our friends. We were also still able to go on and support each other and our children through the terrible losses we endured.

* * *

Once I found I could speak openly about the attack, the shame I'd carried with me was gone. I felt physically lighter, and would encourage anyone who has been through something similar to talk about it. This is not the same as dwelling on one's problems, or making oneself into a victim, it is simply a case of being honest and that is very liberating. Modern attitudes to domestic violence have changed and society has come on a great deal since Erin Pizzey opened that first shelter. You'll find the details of some excellent organisations at the end of this book: they can be contacted in confidence and offer practical help, as well as sympathy and understanding. In my experience just acknowledging the truth can be a huge help.

I sometimes wonder what life would have been like if I had left Colin. Perhaps the children would have been happier – Colin caused a lot of stress in their lives as well as mine. When I've asked them since, they've said they were glad we didn't divorce but I think they also understood that the only way to get through it was for me to find my distance from him, and learn to put myself and them ahead of his endless, taxing needs. That became easier as the children grew older and Colin chose to live more or less permanently away from us in the West Indies. We could live independently, and I had my Norfolk bolthole. Without those advantages, I would probably have had to leave him entirely. As it was, I was able to stay married. I got on with it, and paradoxically grew more confident. It was my choice, which I accept would not be everyone's but I don't regret it. I'm proud that things which may have weakened me, were even intended to destroy me, have in the end made me stronger.

I'm delighted that my children were very lucky in their marriages, but of course it was not just luck: by the time they married it was expected you would get to know very well the person you were about to share your life with before you made your vows. All my sons' wives have been independent, capable women who were brought up to believe, quite rightly, that their opinions carried just as much weight as their husbands'. Of course, all marriages are a negotiation, but they seem to me to be much healthier and happier when both partners enter into those negotiations in good faith and in an atmosphere of equality.

I still love going to weddings and my grandson Cody, son of my eldest child, Charlie, marries in 2022, which delights me, particularly as the ceremony is at Glen, the Tennant family home that has meant so very much to me over the years. Cody has known his lovely fiancée, Rebeka, for nine years and they have lived together for several of those. They met at university and she has a flourishing career of her own. I wish every happiness to them and think they have the best possible chance of a long and wonderful life together.

* * *

As Colin grew older and spent most of his time in the West Indies, he sometimes forgot he could not behave at home as he did in Mustique and St Lucia. I might have changed, but Colin's temper certainly hadn't. One day I was going to Royal Ascot with my dear friend Tim. He, his partner and I were in my flat in London, just getting ready to leave when Colin arrived unexpectedly. He was wearing something Tim admired, and he went to feel the material of Colin's lapel between his fingers, a perfectly innocuous gesture between such old friends. Colin simply whacked him as hard as he could, and threw an absolute fit. My neighbours knocked on the door to see what on earth was going on. Tim's shock was obvious, but his innate good manners meant he didn't respond angrily as he would have been perfectly justified in doing. Once again it was other people's good manners that let Colin off the hook. Now I wonder if part of that violent reaction might have been because Tim is openly gay.

People have often asked me if Colin was gay or bisexual. They were particularly suspicious after his will was read and it was found that he had left everything to Kent, his valet. The innuendo was continual and inescapable. The truth is, I still don't know. Colin was very good with young men and always had male friends whom he mentored and encouraged, but he never gave me any indication that he was sleeping with them. On the other hand I was painfully aware of the multiple affairs he had with women. Perhaps

Colin was bisexual but in his strange way he couldn't bear the idea I might know, and his horror at Tim making even this slight intimate gesture was what had set him off. I remember when I came home that evening, Colin did apologise and say he hoped he hadn't spoiled my day. I told him he could have done, but hadn't, because I simply didn't let him upset me in the way he once had.

The one thing that did begin to change about Colin was his appearance. Ahead of the curve as always, he embraced cosmetic surgery. He had his eyelids lifted and his bags done in his forties and after that he got a taste for it and started having facelifts. When I asked him why, he said that his job was selling land and houses to people and they weren't going to buy anything from a decrepit old man, so he had to stay looking as young as possible. I privately thought that they were very unlikely to trust someone who looked weird and surgically altered. Although his facelifts didn't look too bad, he did get that smooth, waxy sheen to his skin and his lifted eyes looked slightly odd. Later in life, he also had dentures that were a little large for him, so if you weren't used to him, you could find him somewhat startling: smooth skin, lifted eyes and enormous white teeth. Generally, he seemed to heal quite well from his operations but not always. He was staying with me in London after one facelift, so that I could look after him while he recovered. I'd gone out for lunch and when I got back he wasn't there. I went into the bathroom and, to my horror, it was drenched in blood. I nearly fainted on the spot. Off I rushed to the hospital to look for him and there he was, furious. I got an absolute earful. 'Typical!' he shouted. 'You weren't there when I needed you!'

'But, Colin,' I said, jolly relieved to see him alive, and no longer upset by his flashes of temper, 'what on earth happened?'

It turned out his stitches had exploded, or that was what he claimed, but I suspect he had tried to take out one or two himself. I couldn't blame him: he looked like Frankenstein's monster, as if he'd been patched up with thick black thread in a bad blanket stitch. Colin's nasty experience of exploding stitches didn't put him off. He continued to have cosmetic operations, including several more facelifts and tweaks.

'You should get a facelift, Anne,' he told me sometimes. 'Why don't you get your neck done?'

'After your experience, I hardly want an exploding neck!' I replied.

I'm very glad I stuck to my guns and still look relatively normal.

When Colin was dying of cancer, I spent some time looking after him in the West Indies. He wouldn't come back to England for treatment and seeing him so thin and ill was desperately upsetting. One evening after a session at the clinic we went back to where we were staying. We had separate bedrooms with a communicating door and that night I was crying quietly to myself, thinking Colin couldn't hear me. I discovered he could when he came in and climbed into the bed next to me, hugging me tightly. He hadn't done anything like that for years, and almost with surprise said, 'Oh you're quite slim, aren't you, and your skin is so smooth.' It had been so long since he'd touched me, he'd forgotten what I was like. Then he said, 'It wasn't all bad, was it, Anne?'

'No, Colin,' I said. 'Of course not.'

I left soon after that to return to England for a week or two but he died suddenly. I would never see him again. I was devastated and truly mourned him.

Colin provided the sting in the tail, by leaving everything to Kent. I still don't know why he took this awful decision but I experienced it as one last flourish of his sadistic side, the side that revelled in the distress of others and which at times had made any sort of marriage to him seem an impossible burden.

I could not and would not be broken by him from beyond the grave, any more than I would allow it when he was alive. I made a conscious decision not to dwell on that final act of cruelty, and since I made that decision I now see every day as a gift, with my new success to encourage me, and my good health to allow me to enjoy it to the full.

* * *

Despite what I had been taught about what a 'good wife' should be, subservient and uncomplaining, no one should be expected to put up with the treatment I got from Colin. That is a lesson it took me a long time to learn, because it ran counter to so much of my training. No one around Colin should have been expected to deal with the way he behaved either. It is a sad reflection on society that, because of his wealth and family, the position of power he enjoyed in the West Indies, and the feeling of complete entitlement he was brought up with, he got away with so much. Nevertheless I do believe that in the end the person who suffered most was Colin himself. The people he abused in public were no doubt shaken and annoyed, but then carried on with their lives while he lived with his terrible dark feelings every day. Did he ever realise that? I suspect not. Everything that annoyed or upset him was someone else's fault from the first day I met him until the day he died. He always believed absolutely in himself, his abilities, and that without doubt he was the star of every room he walked into. When he was at his best, charming, funny, passionate and brave, he was.

He had enough self-knowledge to know he needed me there, and perhaps one of the reasons he married me was that he saw I had enough courage and resilience to survive and remain married to him no matter what. Our marriage lasted for fifty-four years and now I can look back and feel proud I managed to find a way to stay married to him, and even to agree with him that it wasn't all bad.

CHAPTER FOUR

Hostess

THE GIVING AND receiving of hospitality is a balm and a privilege as well as some of the best fun I've had. I am so glad I learned to love parties rather than dread them, and I'm proud of my role and reputation as a good hostess.

A social life was a necessity as well as a luxury when I was growing up and during my marriage to Colin. Those social events – weekends away, dinners and grand parties – were a way to cement friendships and family ties, entertain dignitaries, introduce interesting people to each other, and were part of showing a confident face to the world. Colin always justified the elaborate parties he held on Mustique as opportunities to enhance the reputation of the island as a glamorous hideaway, which they certainly did, though I don't think that ever quite justified the large amounts of money he spent on them.

I used to love raising money at the charity balls and dinners I organised. My role was to ensure everything went smoothly. For the charity events, I would do much of the organising for the entertainment and decor, but at Glen, our house in Scotland, and on Mustique, my role was much more one of keeping the wheels turning in the background while Colin launched into creating his extravaganzas. If I had married a traditional country-sports-obsessed land-owner, as my father wanted, my entertaining would mostly have consisted of arranging the elaborate shooting lunches and dinners as my mother did so wonderfully for years. Being married to Colin meant the parties were always more fun and unpredictable. It could involve a lot of frantic hard work, but I enjoyed the challenge of entertaining the huge variety of guests we had, from sheikhs to princesses, to film stars and family friends.

The large houses I have lived in were built for grand entertaining as well as being private homes. When I was growing up, I always felt Holkham belonged not just to my family but to everyone, to some degree. This was partly because we had staff living with us, partly because of all the entertaining that went on, particularly after the war, and partly because we always knew that we were only the guardians of the treasures that surrounded us and that our role was to make sure they could be passed on to future generations. Colin's houses, in London and later in Mustique, were designed to be looked at, stages for him to perform on. It's not surprising that the designer Colin liked best, Oliver Messel, primarily worked in the theatre. Colin was a showman, really, an entertainer. Perhaps in another lifetime he would have been a Barnum figure, or the designer of lavish festivities for kings and queens.

My early training stood me in very good stead for this constant social whirl. One should always put the needs of guests first. No matter what else is going on in life, no matter how busy or upset you might be, when the guests arrive you need to keep your chin up and make sure everyone has as much fun as possible. A good guest should be considerate and try to be an asset to any party or occasion. That means dressing well, fitting in with the way a house is run, being appreciative of the hospitality you are offered and joining in as much as possible.

Lots of my early training was designed to prepare me for a life in society which was expected to include entertaining visitors and attending events, from learning the art of making polite, interesting conversation and public speaking at the House of Citizenship, to shadowing all the jobs that existed in a stately home from butler to nursery-maid in Powderham Castle. The Earl and Countess of Devon had set up the scheme as a sort of practical finishing school for young ladies who might expect to run a stately home themselves one day. I rather enjoyed shadowing the butler – we would sneak drinks after serving wine at dinner – but was rather less keen on dealing with dirty nappies when I was shadowing the nursery-maid. Still, it was helpful to have had that experience when I had to run houses myself.

My mother's way of doing things was my model for how guests should be entertained. The credit for a good party or the blame for a bad one was hers, but she did it all brilliantly, even through the years of rationing when keeping up a creditable appearance took a lot of ingenuity. My mother's artistic training meant she had an eye for detail, and though she was very happy in her sailing clothes or motorcycle leathers, she also took great care with her appearance for more public occasions. That was just as important as making sure all the state rooms looked their best.

She organised grand parties, like my coming-out dance and wedding, but the most numerous events were the shooting lunches and weekends. They were all very traditional. Sometimes the lunches at Holkham were just a sandwich, which the guns took with them, but that had to be done properly too. At breakfast a large lunch buffet would also be set out, and each man would make up his own sandwich. The sandwich was then placed in a polished silver lunchbox to be carried up to wherever on the estate they were shooting that day. My mother didn't attend a lot of the dinners she organised as they were male-only affairs, which I think she rather resented. I'm very glad I always got to take part in the parties I helped organise when I was married.

My mother was never a snob and I learned from her how important it is to treat everyone with openness and respect.

Her title might have been grand, but she was friendly and down to earth with everyone, from the King to the maids. She was also very good at making sure we children never got too big for our boots. I'm very grateful for that. Naturally she knew how to address everyone from the Royal Family to bishops and visiting dignitaries, and she never caused offence by being too formal or informal – one could create problems either way. My mother was an example of someone who never put a foot wrong, and I saw how everyone appreciated that, from the Royal Family to the staff and tenants at Holkham. I met a very smart young woman at a talk recently, with mauve hair and a dress covered with rainbows, who curtsied to me. It was very nice of her, and I didn't mind in the slightest, but only the Royal Family are given that distinction. I didn't mention it, I'd hate to make anyone feel uncomfortable, but it did remind me how those rigid rules I learned as a matter of course in my youth are forgotten now. That said, one had to learn to be a bit flexible at times.

Once when I was travelling with Princess Margaret we were invited to visit the Duke and Duchess of Windsor privately for tea at their house in Paris. It was a strange place, cushions embroidered with crowns on them, like the ones in Clarence House, and all the footmen in livery very like that worn in the royal palaces. Even the paintings were all of ancestors and former monarchs, and the whole place was similar to one of the royal residences in London. I thought it was rather sad, as if the Duke was pretending he'd never abdicated at all.

Princess Margaret and the Queen were very fond of their uncle David, but becoming King had put a terrible strain on their father and I'm sure was to blame for his early death. All these circumstances made visiting them a delicate matter. I asked Princess Margaret if I should curtsey to Wallis Simpson, the woman for whom the Duke had abdicated. Princess Margaret was now a senior member of the Royal Family, so she didn't need to curtsey to either of them. The Duke was still 'His Royal Highness', so I would naturally curtsey to him, but Wallis Simpson was explicitly denied that status so it was a tricky bit of etiquette. Princess Margaret said she normally wouldn't advise curtseying, but as we were their guests and it was a private occasion I should go ahead. I'm sure it pleased the Duchess. I was then ushered off to have tea with one of the secretaries, leaving Princess Margaret with the Duke and Duchess.

The house that I ended up running, and where I put into practice what I had learned from my mother, was Glen, the Tennant family home in the Scottish Borders. It's Victorian, rather than Georgian as Holkham is, but I loved it. It is the most enchanting house, with dozens of rooms, turrets and towers, and a sweeping staircase, set in a beautiful valley not far from a loch. When Colin took over in the early sixties, we were united for once in the excitement of bringing the house back from the changes his stepmother had made. We hung William Morris papers, got rid of false walls and revealed the original carved ceilings to bring back its old character. Of course it was Colin who made all the final decisions, but we both loved the late Victorian look that suited the house so well.

I do wish that the producers of the TV series *The Crown* had used the actual house for the scenes they filmed that were supposed to have taken place at Glen. I'm sure they chose the house they used for perfectly good reasons, though it looked rather dismal to me, and it wasn't a patch on the real thing.

Once the decorating was done, we spent many happy times there together as a family, first with the older boys Charlie and Henry, then ten years later with the arrival of Christopher and the twins Amy and May. We had our large family Christmases and Easters there. We'd always have a huge tree, and I found lights and traditional Victorian decorations for it. At Holkham we lit our tree with actual candles, but we had two footmen to stand by and keep an eye on it. In their absence, electric lights were much safer. The night before Christmas, presents were put out under the tree. On Christmas morning, stockings were opened but never before 7 a.m. – that was the rule. I had a large clock outside the bedroom door so the children would know exactly when the opening could begin. Then break-fast was served – porridge followed by scrambled eggs, crispy bacon and roasted tomatoes. After breakfast, we all went to church.

Lunch was always traditional fare of turkey followed by Christmas pudding with sixpences and buttons hidden inside. Nobody ever wanted to get a button in their helping! Lunch was followed by us all sitting around the television to watch the Queen's Speech.

The main presents were opened after a tea of Christmas cake and homemade scones with cream and jam. I will never forget those magical snowy Christmases in our turreted castle, the tree festooned in fairy lights and glass Victorian baubles against a backdrop of sparkling snow.

My main role at Glen, though, was entertaining an enormous number of guests every year, especially during the school and summer holidays, including nannies and children, who were always very welcome. Princess Margaret was a frequent visitor. She wasn't difficult, and in fact easier than many of the other guests, but accommodating royalty and their security was still a challenge. I had to learn to take all these comings and goings in my stride and always did my best to be welcoming, even to the more demanding guests. As we were on the Borders, lots of people would also use us as a halfway house on their way to the Highlands, some even turning up with huge bags of laundry they wanted done.

When Princess Margaret came to stay, I tried to make sure the other guests would be people she liked, or who I thought she would like. When I realised I was a man short for one weekend and invited Roddy Llewelyn at the last minute it turned out I'd managed to invite someone she liked very much indeed. The scandal their relationship caused meant Colin and I were out of favour with the Royal Family for quite some time, but it was worth it to see Princess Margaret happy. It was very strange watching their meeting being dramatised in *The Crown.* They made it look as if I was pimping for her, rather lasciviously pointing out the attractions of the men hanging around the pool. That would be taking being a good hostess a bit too far in my opinion. I suppose it made for a good scene, but it couldn't have been further from the truth. All I did was invite him to stay. The rest was down to them.

The biggest challenge at Glen was learning how to manage not the guests but, inevitably, Colin. He loved amateur theatricals or dramatics and we would put on all sorts of silly shows, as well as regular singsongs round the piano. We all loved the fun of dressing up, but with Colin at the helm it could be exhausting. He'd come up with something he absolutely had to have 'this minute', which we'd discover was only available halfway across the world. The T-shirts printed to look like evening dress for one summer variety show were made only in Los Angeles. Frantic telephone calls, pulling strings and travelling through the night were required to make sure they arrived on time for the performance. They looked amazing, but it was an awful lot of trouble to go to for quite a small, rather inessential element of the proceedings.

I never performed, which I regret now that I've discovered how much I enjoy my public appearances, but Colin told me I was far too valuable for sorting things out backstage. Certainly there was plenty of work to be done. All day long, I would hear my name shouted: 'Anne, Anne! Come here, I need you!' I learned that volunteering to go on a long drive to fetch something Colin had suddenly deemed essential meant a useful escape.

Colin loved our amateur dramatics at Glen so much that he even built a stage in the old drawing room, which is now used as a dining room. There was a large window with a big balcony running outside so people could walk along it and make a grand entrance through the curtain. The people from the village, all of whom worked for Colin, would be summoned as a captive audience, sitting in rows in front of the stage. I would sometimes say to Colin, 'Are you sure they're enjoying it? They're not laughing much.'

'Oh, doesn't matter,' he would reply, with a wave of his hand. 'We just need an audience.'

Goodness knows what they made of it all. I'm afraid I rather failed in my hospitable duties towards them, but the shows didn't last very long and we made sure they were fed and watered for their trouble.

It must have been quite surreal to watch those performances. One show involved several of our male guests dressed in tutus for an impromptu ballet. Our guests, who I think felt obliged to join in as Princess Margaret was so enthusiastic about the project, made a rather odd-looking *corps de ballet*. One, Prince Rupert Loewenstein, the financier who worked with the Rolling Stones for many years, was quite a large man, and another, Michael Szell, a brilliant Hungarian interior designer and dear friend, was painfully tall and balding.

Colin would be so passionate about getting all the details right that there was always a danger he'd have a tantrum. I learned all sorts of ways to prevent that happening, mostly by being extremely non-confrontational while also staying firm, reasonable and unafraid. I also discovered that quickest way out of a bad situation was often to wrongfoot Colin by appearing perfectly fine with whatever demand he made. I think he looked forward to some fireworks and tears, but I often decided I didn't want that particular battle. Besides, it was quite likely that whatever argument we were having would have lasted twice as long if I'd protested, as Colin would have enjoyed it more. I saved a lot of time, energy and emotion by not fighting him on every point.

On holiday in India once we were served our food on large leaves and Colin decided this was marvellous and we should do the same at Glen in the future. I could not imagine what our cook, who served traditional food, often with lashings of gravy, or our butler would think of that, but I simply told Colin if he got the leaves, we'd be happy to try. As was often the case, Colin quickly forgot about this sudden enthusiasm and moved on to something else. If I'd protested too much he could well have dug in his heels and decided leaf service at Glen was absolutely vital. As it was I never did have to break the news to our cook at Glen, or Elio, the butler, that they'd be serving dinner on leaves from now on.

During the day at Glen we would have simple, companionable times with our guests, and go on long walks, which I loved because it gave us time to get to know one another with proper conversations rather than just dinner-party chat. We'd often have picnics, but I learned even a picnic could become a performance. Sometimes the Incredible String Band, who lived on the estate rent-free in exchange for being our in-house band, would play for us. If it looked like rain, Colin would send people off to get large tents set up. Another time he decorated a whole hillside with blue paper flowers. I found the best thing to do was stay cheerful and try to enjoy each moment as it came, taking pleasure from the fun Colin's inventiveness and imagination could add to a weekend party, while avoiding as many storms as possible and making sure our guests were comfortable, well-fed and happy.

It could be frustrating when the staff and I had decided on one thing, then Colin had a sudden idea, which meant we had to change our plans entirely, but there was no point in resenting it. I followed my training, stayed cheerful and put my best foot forward, which made it all much more fun for me and everyone else.

When the shows and singing were over, we could relax in front of the fire with drinks and conversation. And look forward to the next day.

We had an excellent staff, and though I felt terribly busy at the time, I never cleaned a bath or made a bed. Neither did I have to cater for all these guests. I was marvellously well supported so only needed to be front of house. Our excellent cook, Mrs Walker, made my favourite kind of food – solid, unfancy country-house cooking – and our amazing gardens and greenhouses provided lots of wonderful produce. I never had to go near the kitchen, because I could just tick off what we were going to have from the menus Mrs Walker provided and let her do the rest. I was very spoiled, looking back on it now. If I went to someone else's house and enjoyed the food, I'd ask if the cook would give me the recipe to take back to my cook. I'm afraid we all did that.

Now, of course, I wish I'd spent more time watching her in the kitchen, because one thing I never learned was how to cook. I can do the basics like a roast, or kedgeree, and my favourites, such as fish pie, cottage or shepherd's pie, but not a great deal more as I came to it rather late in life. It's probably a legacy of my wartime upbringing, and having traditional nursery food as a child, that I'm still not very adventurous in terms of food, always preferring the familiar options on a menu to anything spicy or unusual. I'd sometimes travel the world to buy things for Colin's parties, but for most of my life I never had to go shopping for food either. At Glen, Mrs Walker would telephone in her orders and the butcher and baker would come to the house in their beautiful old-fashioned vans. If anything was missing one of the garden boys, who could drive, would be sent for it, though it was never referred to as 'shopping'. Whoever went used to say, 'I'll go down for the messages.'

My main role in running Glen, as well as providing a warm and cheerful welcome, was managing the staff and making sure they were as happy as possible. They would often ask me to intercede with Colin, and there were all the usual gripes and problems you might expect from a group of people living and working together. Sometimes the complaints didn't seem very important – 'Lady Glenconner, I don't want to worry you, but the nursery supper was served ten minutes late last night' – but I learned the best thing to do was listen carefully to everyone's concerns no matter what else I was busy with. At least that way everybody got a chance to air their grievances. A little conversation and a cheerful attitude normally provided a solution.

Some of Colin's pet hates made having guests harder than necessary. Even with all the techniques I was learning to manage our lives together, there were occasions when an outburst simply couldn't be avoided. Colin had trigger words that, once uttered, would often produce the most frightful tantrums. One was rather key when entertaining lots of people for dinner. I dreaded saying it but I had to be brave: 'Colin, could you possibly . . . go to the cellar and get some . . .' here it was, the fatal word '. . . *wine?*'

The response was instant. A nerve started twitching in his cheek, his face contorted. 'How *dare* you? Wine? Why the bloody hell do you need some wine?'

'You know very well, Colin . . .'

But it was too late. He was furious, screaming and shouting – it was all my fault, apparently, and why should he do what I wanted? – for an age before he'd finally go down to the cellar and return with a bottle or two that would not now be cold enough by the time we served dinner.

It would have been much easier to get the wine myself, but I wasn't permitted to. Neither was anyone else, although I sometimes cheated and sent the temporary butlers we hired for the summer to fetch it, even though I knew what the result would be. Another furious outburst when Colin saw the wine and realised I'd got round him.

I never knew why wine provoked such a fierce response. Colin never drank it himself, preferring vodka, so perhaps that was it. I suspected he'd once had a fearful experience in the cellar and hated going there. Somehow that dislike grew to cover all wine and in all circumstances.

Though I had a wonderful time at Glen, the need to be always 'on show' could become a strain. Staying cheerful for the family, the staff and our guests, on top of all the changing guest lists, arrivals and Colin's sudden demands could leave me feeling quite exhausted, and I'd learned that feeling like that was not conducive to being a good host and that I also needed time on my own. Despite the size of the house, there was nowhere I could be safe from Colin – he could always track me down – so I bought a small gypsy caravan and had it tucked away in the woods not far from the house. It became my private retreat. Here, in my cosy little caravan with its gingham curtains, comfortable chair and cushions, and a stack of books, I had a secret refuge. Colin couldn't reach me and I had the luxury of an hour or two to myself. When I got back, he might say exasperatedly, 'Anne, where have you been?'

'Just for a walk . . .'

In all honesty he didn't much mind where I'd been, so long as I was now back to sorting out his problems. Having that simple retreat meant I was much better able to look after and enjoy our guests.

In many ways I loved Glen more than Colin did. Once he got used to the balmy climate of the Caribbean, he couldn't bear the cold Scottish weather and he said that being in a valley with only one road out made him feel claustrophobic. As the children got older, he spent less and less time there so I had more holidays at Glen with just the family. The get-togethers were perhaps less exciting when Colin wasn't there, but they were much more relaxing. I still visit, driving myself up to the Borders in my car, though I do stop a few times on the way, these days. It's been one of the great blessings of my life to have enjoyed those happy family times in such a beautiful place, and I am delighted that my grandson Cody and Rebeka have chosen to be married at our Tennant family home. After Charlie and Henry died we had a memorial made for them in a little folly on the way to the loch, which is another place I love to go and remember them. Then I can come back and enjoy the happiness of the house and the family memories it holds.

Our social lives meant arranging and attending all sorts of functions in London and around the country as well as at Glen. Part of being a good guest was being well turned out for every occasion, so I had to learn to dress well and appropriately for each one. When we lived in London in the sixties and seventies, I had a sophisticated wardrobe for our very busy social life and all my charity work. I was expected to go to everything in order to support Colin and so the right clothes, shoes and hats were vital. Even on winter shooting weekends we were still expected to change three times a day, which meant an awful lot of packing. Looking back, it seems extraordinary. I suspect there is less of that, these days, but I know the Royal Family still like to change for dinner.

As I'd grown up during the war, when clothes were rationed, so many changes of outfit were a joy, even if it was quite a lot of fuss. Planning what to wear through the year took a great deal of time, thought and organising. In the summer there was the season, with Ascot and Henley, garden parties and weddings. In the winter, there were shooting weekends, charity dinners and balls. Clothes, fashion and dressing up have played a huge part in my life and I'm lucky enough to have worn some simply wonderful clothes. I might be happiest in my plain skirts and jerseys at home, but I've treasured all the opportunities I've had to wear beautiful evening dresses.

Often I shopped at Bellville Sassoon. My cousin Tom's wife Polly, the Countess of Leicester, is the daughter of Belinda Bellville, who founded the label with David Sassoon. I had a lot of clothes made at their wonderful dress shop, so it was lovely when there was an exhibition at Holkham in honour of Polly's mother. One of my favourite dresses is a Tennant tartan silk evening dress with a family lace collar and cuffs. I also did a lot of shopping at Caroline Charles in Beauchamp Place, and I still do. Her clothes are classic, beautifully made, and they don't go out of fashion. They also suit me, which is the most important thing. If I want something special, I'll go to her. I had a lovely dress and jacket from her for the then Prince of Wales's wedding to the Duchess of Cornwall made of a rose-patterned material with frills around the jacket collar and cuffs. It's fabulous but I've worn it so often I'm not sure how much longer I can go on doing so. Not that I'm frightened of wearing the same thing: people never notice as much as you think they will.

I had a lot to learn from Princess Margaret about clothes. She was always very well dressed and took a great interest in fashion, being artistic herself. She also inspired quite a few trends. She had dressers and maids to help her and once or twice I would see people coming to Kensington Palace with clothes for her, in dress bags, over their arms. The only time I went with her to choose clothes was in New York where we saw Carolina Herrera, who made her some exquisite clothes, and I was lucky enough to be able to choose something from her ready-to-wear collection. We were so lucky to have her as a friend. I always think that one of the most iconic images of Mustique is Robert Mapplethorpe's pictures of Princess Margaret lying on a chaise longue, looking so effortlessly glamorous and beautiful. The Queen, on the other hand, was much happier to be advised on what she wore, and was very lucky to have her talented dresser, Angela Kelly, who made her look fabulous without her having to take too much of a personal interest.

In the sixties there was a huge vogue for wearing wigs and hairpieces. For about a year we ladies wore wigs all the time. I had a very curly one to fulfil my longing as a girl for curly hair, but it made me look like Harpo Marx. I laugh now to think about it, but I still loved it at the time. It was just so quick and easy to put on a wig and there you were, perfect hairstyle in an instant. They were never very popular with hairdressers, though, who kept trying to tell us that they were bad for our hair, but perhaps they liked them less for business reasons. I did try a permanent wave once. Just before my presentation at court, my grandmother gave me one as a present. I went to the hairdresser and my hair was rolled up, then strung with wires and electrified – or that's what it felt like. It took hours and when I came out, my normally quite nice straight. shiny hair was fried to a dry, brittle crisp and bits were falling out. It was mortifying. I ended up going to court looking a bit like a sheep. After that I never regretted a wig or a hairpiece. I still go regularly to the hairdresser for a proper wash and set, especially if I'm going somewhere or meeting someone. It's one of life's pleasures. Perhaps the thing that keeps us looking our best is our hair, and I relish how good all the products are now.

For formal occasions with Princess Margaret we would wear tiaras, which could be rather awkward and often had to be attached to hairpieces. Learning how to manage a tiara was rather fun. Colin bought me a wonderful one, designed with twelve large diamond stars that could also be worn separately as brooches. Once we had a ball and I wore the stars down my bodice like jewelled buttons. May wore the tiara on her wedding day to Anton and it looked simply stunning on her.

I had to have a very different wardrobe on Mustique and it took a while to learn what was best for the climate and the mosquitoes. In the sixties and seventies I had some wonderful kaftans and headscarves to wear there. Our great friend Jinty Money-Coutts used to go to South America and come back with fabulous hand-embroidered dresses she sold to us. I still have some of my lovely kaftans, which is lucky as fashions do come back in style. I wore one in Mustique recently that I bought fifty years ago and everyone wanted to know where I'd got it.

As well as entertaining our friends and attending private parties, it was expected that ladies of my background would do a great deal of charity work. I learned to love that side of my entertaining career and my position in the Royal Household enabled me to see how much marvellous charity work is done throughout the country and how vital the support of the Royal Family is. I found it fascinating to see close up what needed to be done, and I was very glad to be able to do some of this work myself. It was hugely rewarding to be involved with some wonderful organisations, and to be able to help those less fortunate than myself. I also felt it was my duty to do whatever I could to repay some of my own good fortune.

Alongside helping Erin Pizzey in the early days of Refuge, I was involved in the National Rheumatoid Arthritis Society, the National Association of Maternal and Child Welfare, and was president of the disability-equality charity now known as Scope, so I arranged many events and fundraisers. It was hard work but enormous fun as well. The important thing was to make it a really splendid occasion so people would not only be enthused about the charity, but have a really good time. I learned people tend to be far more generous when they are enjoying themselves.

I organised dozens of events, fetes, theatre revues and dinners, and met all sorts of people, including stars of stage and screen who kindly gave their time for free. A good guest list, a strong theme, and an element of silliness always helped make these occasions special. Everyone got the chance to dress up and have fun, and the charities got the funds to do their valuable work as well as plenty of positive press attention. One of my favourite moments came when I was organising a pro-am golf tournament for Scope and Bob Hope played. I have a huge photograph of the two of us, one of my most treasured possessions. Vera Lynn supported the children's hospital that the charity managed, and many other kind people helped, including Sir Roger Moore and Sir John Mills.

One of my favourite parties in aid of charity involved no dressing up or celebrity appearances, and no complicated preparations. It was Colin's idea, and it was a stroke of genius. When we bought our house in Tite Street, Chelsea, and realised that as it was it couldn't be saved, we turned the demolition of the interior into a party. For a donation to the National Rheumatoid Arthritis Society, our guests were invited to come and let rip. No fancy outfits were required, just old clothes, a hard hat and some safety spectacles, which we provided. No props, except for a hammer or a mallet and some spray cans of paint. And no construction. Just destruction.

It was thrilling. We were allowed to do exactly what we wanted and I'd never felt so liberated. Lots of friends and family came. We put out tables of food and drink where they wouldn't get contaminated by dust, and played very loud music on a tape recorder, which seemed to encourage people to let loose as the noise thundered through the house. They smashed everything up, knocked holes in walls, destroyed cupboards. Everyone behaved like complete hooligans. The glass was particularly satisfying to smash, and all the mirrors were hammered into shards. As for the graffiti . . . Well, it was certainly interesting to see what people drew when they didn't care and knew it wouldn't last. I said to Colin, 'I've always longed to write the word "fuck" and now I can.' I sprayed it across a wall with my paint tin, feeling very reckless and rude. I'm afraid it was far from the rudest thing that got sprayed on the house that day. Everyone went potty and though the place was an absolute wreck, people felt as though they had never had such a fun time. The last person to leave was Colin's mother. She was still madly bashing things when everyone else had gone, absolutely gleeful with it. I believe there are now places you can pay to visit which allow you to demolish things, like old televisions and stereos and coffee-tables. I know first-hand how satisfying a bit of destruction can be so, once again, Colin was ahead of his time.

I discovered it wasn't necessary to be buttoned up and perfect, in the way I'd become used to, and that lavishness was not the only ingredient for a good party. It was a lesson I certainly took to heart, though Colin didn't, as his parties on Mustique proved.

When Colin first bought the island, we had to warn anyone brave enough to join us that accommodation was rather different from what they might expect at Glen. I learned the best thing to do was to make sure people knew exactly what to expect. A good host makes sure people don't get any nasty surprises. As a result, early visitors understood what the conditions were and accepted them cheerfully. We lived in the most basic way, without running water or electricity, sleeping without proper beds and fighting off mosquitoes while we survived on endless fish and not much else. Even after several years, Mustique was still very basic, and the contrast between that and my life as a lady in waiting – attending state banquets, travelling on the Queen's Flight, staying in palaces and government residences – struck me as funny.

I admit I didn't think I'd be able to put up with life on Mustique for long in those early years. The bare, barren scrub of the island when it was wild was not very promising, despite the beautiful beaches and the warm sea. There were a few acres devoted to growing cotton, and some almost impassable thickets of trees, but not a great deal else. Wild cattle and goats rampaged around in an alarming fashion, eating what little vegetation there was. I couldn't see the appeal at all when we first arrived – the whole island felt sunburned and dry. Our early visitors tended to be ones with a sense of adventure. When Princess Margaret first came with her husband, they arrived on the Royal Yacht *Britannia*, and they welcomed us on board, letting us have a luxurious bath then giving us dinner. In return we gave them a tour of the island – riding on a bench strapped to a trailer and towed by a tractor. Obviously it didn't put Princess Margaret off, as she accepted Colin's offer of a piece of land on the island with alacrity and visited us several times before her beautiful house, Les Jolies Eaux, was built.

Colin developed the island, bringing in running water and replanting the whole place so it became the paradise it is today. He cultivated grass, planted coconuts and sea cotton, and controlled the wild animals. Eventually, with a supply of fresh water and as the planting matured, beautiful gardens were created. I began to love it for the glorious sense of peace it could bring and the natural beauty and scents of the marvellous plants and flowers, so different from what I'd known back in Norfolk. It made a magnificent backdrop for all the entertaining we did. However difficult Colin was at times, I can't help admiring what he achieved on Mustique. The vision was all his.

By the time Colin was throwing the great balls for his fiftieth and sixtieth birthdays, the island looked wonderful. Lots of extraordinary houses were being built and Basil's Bar, the social hub of the island, was well established, but I was beginning to resent the huge amounts of money that Colin was spending on the parties. It was one thing to spend so much on the island – those were investments that would improve everybody's lives for generations to come – but to throw away thousands and thousands on something as ephemeral as a party was not the same. Colin gave parties that were so lavish and lasted so long that they were more like festivals. They took a great deal of planning, then ages to recover from and tidy up after.

His fiftieth-birthday invitations included the air fare to Mustique, accommodation and a week's worth of parties culminating in the famous Golden Ball, with everyone dressed from head to foot in gold, and oiled boys, providing a very striking sight indeed. Colin had met Robert Mapplethorpe in New York – he was just starting his career as a photographer – and invited him to capture the party, which he did in such style, creating some of the most iconic images of Mustique. Lots of the guests were our family and friends, but the fact that Mick and Bianca Jagger and Princess Margaret were among them gave the party the mix of royal and celebrity glamour that made Mustique such a byword for decadence in the years to come. Colin's parties had to be over the top, astonishing and wildly impressive, like something from the royal courts of centuries past. Each one had to be better than the last.

He loved colour. We all did. The swirling psychedelia of the sixties was no doubt a reaction to the drabness of our wartime childhoods. Nevertheless, these explosions of colour and extravagance on Mustique gave me as much unease as enjoyment. Colin told me that they would make Mustique famous, which they did, and bring in more investors, which they did, but that never replaced the vast amounts of money lavished on them. I couldn't rein him in much, so I decided the only thing to do was enjoy it as much as I could and make sure everyone else did too. Still, Colin was so obsessive about the details he would exhaust himself and everyone else in the run-up to these grand occasions. He needed an injection from the doctor before the ball just to get him through the party.

None of that put him off. His sixtieth birthday was two years in the planning and was even more glamorous and extravagant than his fiftieth, including trips to India to

buy clothes for all our guests and huge, beautifully decorated tents. The enormous sailing ship *Wind Star* was
rented for extra accommodation and the festivities included
lunches, dinners, treasure hunts and games, and culmin-
ated in the Peacock Ball. I wonder what happened to all
those wonderful costumes and headdresses now. I rather
wished he could have remembered that this sort of extravagance was unnecessary. I had learned that all one really
needs for an excellent party is good people, music and
enough food and drink to go round. That was true on
Mustique too. It sometimes seemed the dancing would
never end. Anyone who came to the island could expect
to be pulled into a conga around the beach at the very
least. Most days, we'd meet on one of the beaches for
lunch or supper. Supper was often fresh fish wrapped in
seaweed and grilled over a fire, then unwrapped and sprin-
kled with lime juice.

In the evenings, there was always music, singing and
dancing, and those informal parties under the Caribbean
stars were some of the happiest of times, when we could
relax and dance our hearts out. And many hearts were
joined and broken on the dance-floors of Mustique at those
fabulous parties.

I still go out to Mustique when invited by my great friend
Josephine Loewenstein, to revisit the familiar places and
remember how it used to be when Colin took the risk of
buying it. I'm so lucky still to be able to enjoy the fabulous

place it is now, and I hope I have a few more years to come of enjoying it. I was touched that, after Prince William's wedding, a replica of Basil's Bar was created at the Goring Hotel, where Catherine stayed the night before her wedding, to mark the couple's connection with Mustique and the happy times they spent there. Colin, the great party maestro, would have been thrilled.

Colin loved being the star of these parties, and his imagination and flair certainly made them memorable. He also had a talent for finding interesting people so our guests knew that they would always enjoy good conversation. He often needed me there to help him, which was not surprising, given he was incapable of thinking about other people's needs at times.

Colin had quite odd tastes, and was prone to fixations, obsessions and eccentricities. For example, he never touched coffee after going to Trinidad to sample the coffee for his family business. That experience put him off completely. He ate strange things, often out of paper bags, such as jellied eggs, and in the end seemed to go off food altogether, eating mostly huge avocados and tropical fruit. It never occurred to him that his guests might have other ideas about food. In his last house in St Lucia, he stayed true to form and didn't have a kitchen, only a fridge – not even a toaster by then. Our friend Zanna went to stay with him and Colin had only cranberries and ice in the fridge. She was given so little food that she fainted on the way home.

It was not just Colin who, I felt, broke the rules of being a good host sometimes. At one point in the sixties, everyone seemed to be smoking pot or weed all the time and it was going round at every dinner party we went to. Everywhere seemed to smell of it. Colin didn't show much interest in dabbling, although I think he might have tried something once or twice – and I believe he spiked my drink that time in the Grenadines. I don't think he really needed any more stimulation, so I'm grateful he didn't. I was never tempted by drugs – they didn't make people any more interesting to talk to as far as I could see.

Once we were at a friend's birthday party, however, and it turned out that the cake had been baked with pot. No one told me and I ate a large lump of it, thinking it was a date. I began to act quite strangely and Colin, to his credit, noticed and guessed what had happened. He took me home at once and put me to bed, where I had the most appalling experience, watching blood dripping from the walls and bed curtains. I had to stay there for three days before I was well enough to get up. That completely put me off and I made sure never to touch anything like it again. Colin was very angry with them for providing a drugged cake. And he was right to be. It certainly ran against my rule of making sure guests don't get any nasty surprises.

Even Princess Margaret didn't get it right all the time. I remember one embarrassment when she had invited some American friends to London during the weekend of the

Royal Wedding of Prince Charles to Lady Diana Spencer. They had been extremely generous to Princess Margaret and were thrilled to be invited to the biggest event in decades. On the morning of the Royal Wedding, they came downstairs in the most lovely outfits, ready to accompany Princess Margaret to St Paul's Cathedral, but just as she was leaving, she simply called behind her, 'Oh, good, there you are. The television is on in the drawing room for you to watch and there are some sandwiches if you want them.'

I couldn't hide how I felt when she told me about this, and said frankly that it was very awkward to have left them there. Princess Margaret said crossly, 'It's ridiculous, Anne. How could they possibly have thought they were going to the wedding?'

But they had thought they were.

I suspect that she had believed she could invite them, but at some point had been told there weren't enough invitations so either forgot to tell her friends, or was too proud to admit she couldn't invite them after all. Whichever it was, she handled it badly. Even princesses occasionally need to know when they've been rude, and I think, though cross, she accepted my admonition. It's testament to the generous character and amazing good manners of her guests that they never told anyone about it, or held it against her but continued to be her good friends for many years.

I'm sure I made mistakes too, but I've enjoyed all these parties over the years. Giving them also taught me what a pleasure it can be to clean up. Perhaps it wouldn't appeal as much if I had to do it all the time, but I honestly think in another life I might have been a housekeeper or perhaps the matron in a hospital. I do love to restore order. It gives me a great sense of comfort and security. Beds neatly made with sharp corners make me happy. I think Princess Margaret was similar: she liked nothing better than putting on her Marigolds and getting on with a bit of cleaning. Virtually the first thing she would do when she arrived at my house was clean my car. I was always finding her up a ladder or dismantling something to clean.

I've also learned I liked to be tucked away somewhere, feeling safe. My favourite places in all those grand houses were always attics or high-up rooms. Perhaps it comes from having spent so much time with the servants and in the attics of Holkham when I was a child. Those were private spaces, not like the public parts of the house, so perhaps that's what I was looking for when I retreated to them, some privacy where I didn't have to think about anyone's comfort but my own. When I was staying in Kensington Palace, I loved the feeling of being hidden away with everything I needed. I had my large bed-sitting room with its own tiny kitchen on the top floor and that was such a nice feeling.

I'm always searching for that sense of cosy comfort and luckily my home in Norfolk and my London flat both offer it. Perhaps it stems from Billy Williams finding secret places just for me all those years ago to recover from the stress Miss Bonner caused. Perhaps it was a coping mechanism for my noisy, tumultuous marriage. Perhaps it was even a response to a life lived often on show in one way or another. For whatever reason, I found that although I had learned to enjoy parties, I also needed private corners where I could gather my thoughts in peace before heading out into the social fray again.

Even in dark times, taking the time to celebrate can be a very good idea. Amy and May had their coming-out dance in 1988, after Christopher's accident and Henry's diagnosis, but before Charlie married. It was a wonderful party and we threw ourselves into making it as much fun as possible. Coming-out dances were very old hat by that time – there were no dance cards, and no vetting of the guests to weed out undesirable suitors, but we still wanted to celebrate our daughters. We were at Hill House and turned the garden into a slice of paradise with lights in the trees and a steel band to bring a little of the Mustique magic to London. All our friends and theirs came in spectacular colourful outfits and it was a chance for us to be together and enjoy what we had. We must have been having fun, as the neighbours eventually sent the police round to complain about the noise – that was a problem we never had to deal with at Glen or on Mustique.

Nowadays I prefer a lunch party to grand parties in the evening, but I'm lucky enough to be invited out to some lovely places and enjoy some very glamorous times. Book events sometimes involve lunch or dinner, which is an excellent chance to meet my hosts and fellow authors. I'm so lucky to have a career now that introduces me to new friends.

I might not enjoy dinner parties quite as much any more but I make an exception for the Prince of Wales, our new King, who is sometimes kind enough to ask me for dinner at Sandringham when he is there. He very sweetly sends a car so that I don't have to drive at night, which I'm less fond of doing these days. But, more than ever, I've learned my idea of a brilliant time is a cosy weekend at home with close friends or my family. I love a brisk walk, a delicious lunch or early supper, good wine, lots of conversation and a great deal of laughter. Everyone should feel looked after and comfortable, but not bossed about or on their best behaviour. Absolutely nothing could be nicer, because you get to know people properly in convivial and relaxing surroundings. I know there are those who love a cocktail party, but I'm afraid I think those gatherings are the worst. A mass of people in a room, shouting, so you can't hear anything, then someone looking over your shoulder to see if there is anyone better to talk to. After two painful hours going hoarse and trying to get a drink, it's over.

No. Give me a country weekend. It's more work if you are the one doing the entertaining, but it's the best. Home comforts, in the end, are the nicest. You'll never regret the happy times you spend with friends and family.

Some exceptions have to be made, though, and some occasions demand a slightly grander celebration. Everyone needs to mark the milestones in the journey and the companions on our travels. If life has taught me anything it is that sometimes it is very important to stop and say, 'Isn't life wonderful? I'm so glad you're here to share it with me.'

I didn't have large parties for my birthdays the way Colin did, but I think my ninetieth went some way to redress the balance. Tom and Polly, the Earl and Countess of Leicester, were kind enough to lend me Holkham, so I had the chance to celebrate this landmark in my childhood home, surrounded by memories of my family and with friends old and new. It was a lunch party, so the older people like myself could enjoy it properly. Everyone had the chance to look round the state rooms and enjoy a drink on the Portico, before we ate in the Statue Gallery. I'd had a lovely time planning the menu with lots of delicious local produce, and arranging the seating so that everyone could enjoy themselves. Planning an event like that was quite a challenge, but I was determined to enjoy every moment of it, and I had lots of help from Johanna, Christopher's wife, the twins and the wonderful staff and family at Holkham, all of whom know the skills of holding an excellent party.

Holkham was blessed with a beautiful sunny day – in fact Holkham was the star of the occasion, so all my guests got to see it at its finest, just as another group had on the day of my coming-out dance almost seventy years before. I feel so lucky to have been able to celebrate this milestone surrounded by so much love and kindness. I had a hard act to follow in Colin, but this time it was my party and I hope that everyone enjoyed it even half as much as I did.

Gatherings I attend far more often these days are funerals, which I suppose are the last public event of one's life. I do have plans for mine. My close friends Zanna and Nicky Johnston died recently and had a wonderful joint funeral, so appropriate after a long life together. It was terribly poignant. Their wicker coffins sat side by side at the front of the church, one topped with Zanna's favourite hat, and the other with Nicky's. Their daughters spoke beautifully and at the end, as the coffins were taken out, a man with a wonderful voice sang 'Wish Me Luck As You Wave Me Goodbye'. That was it for me, I was in absolute floods. It was terribly moving. But that is what funerals are for, to celebrate a life and allow us to grieve – and a good one will provide that opportunity for everyone who attends. I hope that will be the same at mine. When I see a really good idea at a funeral that I think would be rather lovely to have at mine, I add it to my list. When I mention yet another suggestion to the children, they roll their eyes and say, 'Mum! You've got pages and pages of these! At this rate, the funeral will go on for days.'

What I'd really like is to be sent off on a small burning boat, out onto the sea. But I don't think they allow that in this country. I'll just have to whittle down my ideas and settle on what I really want.

In the meantime I'll go on enjoying my friends and family for as long as I can, entertaining them in Norfolk and London and visiting them in return.

CHAPTER FIVE

Mother

ONE OF THE hardest roles in my life has been as a mother. It has taught me a great deal about love, suffering, redemption, gratitude and grace. I've learned how lucky I could be, as well as how much I could endure.

I was blessed to be the mother of five amazing children, and I buried two of them while caring for my third son as he recovered from a terrible head injury. To anyone who is suffering through anything similar I send my love and prayers. I understand just how desperate the depths of grief can be.

My children have also been the source of the greatest happiness in my life. Though I lost Charlie and Henry, I now get to love their children and grandchildren. Christopher has gone on to lead a full and happy life, and my twin daughters, Amy and May, make me incredibly proud every day. I am so glad to have had them at my side during my new life as an author.

I've always loved children and loved being a mother, a grandmother, and now feel very lucky to be a great-grandmother. Family is deeply important to me, the bedrock of my existence. Now that I am watching my own children and grandchildren parent, it has made me try to see afresh the whole wonderful, messy, painful and happy experience of motherhood.

This has not always been easy for me. Losing Charlie and Henry has often made me focus on what went wrong, and the impulse to punish myself for mistakes is strong. I learned that for my own survival I had to fight against that impulse. I wish I could go back and do things differently, but I can't and nothing I can do will change that. My faith has taught me to forgive others and myself, and that has led to an acceptance that has made it possible for me to love life again after losing Charlie and Henry. At times I have been very angry, and at times the sadness has been overwhelming, but the love of my surviving children and my friends has taught me to treasure my memories, and think of the laughter and joy I shared with my boys rather than the pain of losing them. Writing about Charlie and Henry in *Lady in Waiting* and again here, especially about their deaths, has left me in floods of tears, but I hope that my story shows it is possible to survive even these terrible events and celebrate those we have lost, their legacy, and all our happy memories.

* * *

I had Charlie when I was still very young in 1958 having got pregnant on our honeymoon. I hadn't yet learned how to deal with Colin at all. It was, to say the least, a difficult start to motherhood. In addition to Charlie's sleeping problem, I knew I wanted to breastfeed but hadn't realised what a challenge that would be. The monthly nurse helped me to get on track – I was lucky to have her – but Charlie had reflux, a horrible condition when the milk comes back up, so feeding him was very difficult no matter how hard I tried.

Apart from the lack of any real information on what to expect in pregnancy and through the process of birth, our counselling after the birth was largely about the need to get back into good shape and restart our sex lives as soon as possible for the sake of our husbands. As always husbands came first, children second. That was what I had learned from my earliest days, even though everything I was feeling now told me it was wrong. Colin was a particularly difficult man, I know, but that principle was generally accepted. As a result I thought my instincts must be wrong and that everyone else must be right. It was one lesson from childhood that seemed to be serving me badly rather than well.

A lot of new mothers put themselves under so much strain. We all have a desire to be perfect and when we're not, and neither is our baby, we feel miserable. I had one very strict book that gave me a rigid timetable with absolutely no flexibility and that didn't seem to do anything for Charlie. Now any number of books are devoted to raising children, as well as websites and forums and frank discussions on television and radio about how hard and demanding motherhood is. What a relief it would have been to hear something like that. If those resources had been available in my day, I would probably have met dozens of mothers with fractious babies like mine, and felt comforted that it wasn't just me feeling like a failure. I would have learned more about Charlie's reflux problem and how to treat it, and would have known that, however hard it was, it would stop eventually. I was desperate, thinking it would go on for ever. With more information, I would probably have learned helpful techniques to get Charlie to sleep too. Years later, poor May suffered in the same way when her second daughter had reflux and didn't sleep for the first three months. Terrible as it was, we knew a lot more about how to cope with it, and May got lots of support and learned to express breast milk so she could control feeding a little more.

It would all have been so liberating for me and my friends to free ourselves from Nanny's routines. If you and your baby thrive on routine, excellent. Get a good one in place. I know there are still strict nannies who advocate timetables and naughty steps and have used those techniques to help children and young mothers, but they don't work for everyone. If something more relaxed suits you and your baby, do that instead. My grandson Euan's wife had her babies attached to her all the time in slings and did on-demand feeding and relaxed bedtimes and that seemed to work very well for them. If I'd even thought to do such a thing, Colin would never have allowed it and would have thought I'd gone completely mad. Everyone we knew was following the traditional route so I did my best to do the same.

Women have more choices now, and they don't have to make it all look easy any longer. I think that would be an important lesson for any mother to learn: you don't need to pretend everything is fine. I wish I had learned it. It seemed that I was getting it all wrong, even though I thought I was doing what was expected of me: I had my nanny; I was putting my husband first; I was breastfeeding; I had bought the right cot. I felt that it was my fault, especially when Nanny White arrived on the scene and seemed to have more success with quieting and comforting Charlie than I did, which was very depressing.

Charlie loved Nanny White so I, feeling rather sad and despondent, tried not to get in the way and told myself that leaving him to her care was for the best.

My mothering skills hadn't improved a great deal by the time Henry arrived three years later. He weighed in at an enormous eleven pounds so it took a while to recover from that exceptionally difficult and painful birth. I was told I might never have more children, which was a great sadness to me. It was in the midst of that period that Colin sacked

Nanny White, devastating Charlie and making him resent his new brother terribly. I breastfed Henry for a while and then did what I thought was right. Put my husband first and ceded control of the nursery to the new nanny.

Until the children reached their early teens, the nannies controlled the nurseries and, in matters of child-rearing, we deferred to them, learned their preferred routines and went obediently along with everything they said. After all, they were the experts, we were just the mothers. As such we rarely got a look-in and we weren't terribly inventive in terms of breaking the mould of tradition. We all had the same kit and dressed our children in the same way. All the babies had beautiful nightdresses, very long, made of winceyette and fine cotton, embroidered, with sashes. The day gowns were cotton or linen. The nannies and their friends knitted matinee jackets or little crossover cardigans, mittens and hats, and they were sent as arrival gifts, adding to the babies' identical looks. As soon as they could move, boys wore romper suits, with lovely fat, puffy bottoms. Prince Andrew was born at about the same time as Henry, and the Queen and I exchanged letters and romper suits, both our boys in the same uniform of the day.

I have no idea now why letting the nannies rule the roost was what we had to do, but I had always been taught that conformity was everything and individuality was not important so I thought I was raising the boys in the correct way. I'm very glad that's changed: parents these days are much better at saying what they want for their children and there is much more concern for their individual needs. The nannies were hidebound by their own rules and traditions, and hugely aware of status. They were called by the name of the family they were working for and had a very strict hierarchy. One of the nannies took her own pram wherever she went and painted it with the crest of her new family, as she was never with anyone less than a lord. In the park, they had their own benches allocated: dukes' nannies, marquesses' nannies, earls' nannies and so on. It sounds rather absurd now, but it was all very important to them. The nannies even looked the same, in grey coats and hats and white gloves.

They also had control over what the children wore as they grew up, including shopping for them, and they all went down the same conventional route. The little girls generally had blue Viyella dressing-gowns with rabbits on them, and in their pre-school years, they would have beautiful little Hayford coats with pearl buttons and velvet collars, with a dart at the back so that they looked immaculate. Then, as they got bigger, they moved into Jaeger coats. Our job as mothers was just to vet the final choices and write the enormous cheques, then go on with our lives. I remember going into the shops, sitting down with a cup of tea and being shown all the lovely things my nanny had chosen. I have to admit, it was great fun, almost like selecting costumes for a play, even if it did make the business of dressing the children rather remote. They liked their charges to look smart and expensively dressed, as it reflected well on them. The children had no say at all. I still find it a novelty to see children dictating what they will or won't wear, and throwing tantrums if they don't get their own way. I disapprove of tantrums, or over-indulging children's whims but I do like the more individual relaxed way of dressing. As a great tree-climber myself, I would have loved to wear jeans and dungarees instead of kilts and jerseys.

I was fighting my own instincts to spend more time with the older boys, but still following convention. Nor did I question that the boys would go away to prep school and boarding school. For us, nearly all boys went to prep school and then Eton, unless they failed the entrance exam, which was what happened in Charlie's case. Eton, we believed, would shape the boy into a man. There was no thought that you might find the school that suited the boy's character, or not send them away at all. I certainly believed that sending the boys away to school when they were still very little was quite normal and I didn't object even if I hated waving goodbye to them. I hate crying, and try to avoid doing so, but we'd all end up in floods as I drove them to school at the beginning of term. We loved our children and wanted them to be happy, so we did our best to set them up for their adult lives. We accepted as an absolute truth that school would solve their problems and shape them into happy and functional adults. I can't think why we believed this, when many of the men we knew who'd gone down this route had been so damaged by it, but we did, without question. What the children were actually like didn't really come into it.

These days, children are not sent away quite as young as they once were and often not at all, and boarding schools seem to have a great deal more concern for their welfare and the suitability of the staff, with background checks and so on. They look like very jolly places to be and those who are lucky enough to be sent to a good boarding school seem to have a wonderful time. Parents are also much more likely to get involved with what's happening at school, and to speak up if they think things are going wrong. There seem to be lots of parent-teacher meetings, and far more communication than we ever had with our children's schools. Issues are flagged early. That must be good. I'm sure it would have helped Charlie if that had been the case in his day.

Sometimes I wonder if society isn't moving a little too far towards being overly focused on children and their needs. Some of them seem to have everything done for them to the extent that they are failing to learn how to grow up and cope for themselves. Children need to learn how to cope with the ups and downs of life. I wonder if it's ever possible to get it right. It's hard work finding the balance so that children are protected and cared for, and given enough independence to become self-sufficient. Even though we followed the rules of our day, relying on nannies and sending the children away to school to learn to be self-sufficient young men, we didn't get it right with Charlie but Henry loved his prep school and Eton.

They were both creative, charming and charismatic, and I adored them, but Charlie never really learned to look after himself or take responsibility for his own life. Colin continued to fund both of them and Charlie never had a proper job. Perhaps if we had forced them to be independent sooner, they might have taken more responsibility for themselves, made better choices and that would have changed the outcome. But Charlie began taking heroin at the age of sixteen, though we didn't know that for a long time afterwards. Henry found out he was HIV positive when he was only twenty-six.

In the early years, Colin was not someone I could share the burden of parenthood with at all. In later years, he and I worked together more as a team, when we had to face some tremendous challenges. To give him his due, he did his best to be understanding. When Charlie couldn't bear his prep school, Colin let him come home and go to a day school. Charlie was already showing some strange quirks and ideas that would haunt him for years. Now I realise he would be diagnosed as having obsessive compulsive disorder, but though we did take him to a psychiatrist the only diagnosis offered was neurosis, and there was no further help. We both knew plenty of eccentrics – Colin's family was full of them – so we thought the best thing to do was accept Charlie as he was and not make a fuss. Our friends did the same when Charlie was playing out one of his strange obsessive rituals, and we'd all just let him get on with it without comment: we felt that drawing attention to it or making a fuss would just distress him. We thought we were learning the best way to look after him and being kind.

Almost ten years after Henry's birth, my doctor let me know that there had been significant medical advances so if I wanted more children I could have them. I didn't think twice about going ahead, and not long after that Christopher was born. That was when our new nanny, Barbara Barnes, arrived. She was wonderful and made such a difference to our lives, helping me to be a much more confident mother.

By this time I had learned how to cope much better with being married to Colin, and with Barbara's support and approval I was able to involve myself more with Christopher rather than defer to an intimidating old-fashioned nanny, who acted like I had no right to interfere. When the shooting season started, with its long weekends away, I decided not to give up breastfeeding, as I had with the older boys, but simply ask our friends if I could bring Christopher and Barbara with us. I wouldn't have dreamed of doing so before, but learned to my delight it was very straightforward just to ask. They were all very accommodating, and in fact it turned out to be tremendous fun having the baby there, with everyone cooing over him. Christopher was so heavenly, always giggling and smiling, and everyone loved him. And I could escape to see him and feed him, which was wonderful for me. I remember that period very happily and wish I'd had it with the older boys.

It was only when I had Christopher, who was so easy, ate everything, loved everything, and slept like an angel, that I learned quite how difficult life with Charlie had been when he was little. I wonder now how much my own anxiety and moods had affected him and exacerbated his difficulties.

It was ironic that, having been a 'disappointing' girl myself, I seemed able to produce only boys. Much as I adored Christopher, who was sunny and delightful from the start, I also longed for a girl and hoped that the next pregnancy might be the one. I got pregnant again fairly quickly, but there were no early scans for me to discover what I was going to have. It was only a week before the birth, when I was given an X-ray to find out why the baby's head hadn't yet engaged, that the nurse delivered some astonishing news.

'Oh, Lady Glenconner, you're having twins!'

I think she was rather surprised when I burst into tears of woe. I was huge – it turned out I was carrying twelve pounds of baby: the twins were six pounds each. I was already so tired with my vast bump and I didn't have two of anything. Luckily one of my friends said, 'Don't worry, I'm coming round in a taxi and bringing everything you need: a Moses basket, a cot and another set of clothes.' It was so kind of her. I'd been worried I'd have to put one of the babies in a drawer, like Babar the Elephant.

I went into labour with the twins on a Sunday and as I was thirty-eight, which was considered old in those days, my obstetrician had said he wanted to be present at the birth. When I arrived at the hospital, labour was already well under way and I could tell the babies were going to be born quite quickly. The house doctor said, 'Could you possibly wait and not push? Your consultant wants to be at the birth but he's playing tennis and will be here in about half an hour.'

In the end I got very cross and said, 'I don't care. I can't wait. I'm going to push!' And just at that moment he came running in, still dressed in his tennis clothes, in time to pull out the first baby. He held up May and said, 'You've got one daughter . . . And . . .' five minutes later '. . . another daughter!'

Oh, the relief. And now not one but two much-wanted daughters. His duty done, he went back to his game. I can laugh now but really it was outrageous to be asked to delay giving birth for the sake of a tennis match. The birth process was very medicalised, mostly overseen by men, and of course their needs came first. This was in 1970, and that hadn't changed. I'm glad a woman gets a good deal more say now about what happens to her during the birth. After all, she is the one having the baby.

These days, there are no mysteries about how babies are conceived and the whole process is explained in great detail. My daughter May went to childbirth classes with her husband Anton and they put a lot of time and thought into preparing. It was just as much Anton's responsibility as May's. He intended to be with her every step of the way and it was a shared experience. I think most women today must feel a great deal more supported and informed than we were.

I was so lucky to be able to conceive naturally, though the years when I thought I couldn't have any more children for medical reasons were terribly painful, even though I had two beautiful sons. IVF is a wonderful advance for the couples of today who are having problems with fertility. Not only was infertility a source of great pain for those of my generation, it was also not talked about directly, and rarely with those involved, especially as it was generally assumed to be the woman's fault. Back then, it felt like a silent stain that one should be ashamed of. It's another great improvement that so many are able to experience the joy of parenthood who otherwise would not.

When my daughter May had her own babies, I was thrilled. It was a marvellous experience to help in her new motherhood, and to have the joy of being a grandmother again. May had the rather unusual experience of having advance warning of going into labour. Amy rang her up and said, 'Have you started having contractions? Because I have.'

'But I'm the one having the baby!' May said. Sure enough, she started her contractions not long after. The girls had always experienced things at exactly the same time, and had sympathetic pains, so it really wasn't a surprise. They are mirror twins, and have been incredibly close all their lives. At one point they told us they wanted to go to separate schools, which we agreed to arrange. I thought it was terribly brave of them, and it was hard for them at first but I'm glad they found a way to be apart as well as together.

Once Barbara Barnes came into my life, things began to improve for all of us and I learned how to find and maintain a new balance in our lives between the children's needs, my needs and Colin's. She was so refreshing. Her job was a career for her, she was clever and knowledgeable, and her brilliance as a nanny was shown by how happy and stable Christopher, Amy and May were. Even Colin listened to Barbara, and he said that if she had looked after Charlie and Henry, things might have been very different. Barbara had a mind of her own. She wasn't known as Nanny Tennant but just as Barbara. She didn't wear traditional nanny uniform, and she sat on whichever bench she wanted, even if that did take a bit of sorting out with other households and nannies. Barbara was not so set on traditional outfits either, and in the seventies the children spent their summers in jeans and jumpers, and on Mustique, it was shorts, T-shirts and swimming things. Much more relaxed all around.

Finally, I learned it was perfectly acceptable for me to have a mind of my own too. When it came to the nursery of the London house, and Colin was diverted with another project, I chose the decoration. Everyone had the idea of a perfect nursery – a cosy room with a fire and a fender to warm the nightclothes on – but I thought that what the children most needed was somewhere to play so my nursery had a smart lino floor and a rug, and quite modern furniture. My friends were rather shocked that it broke all the conventions, a peculiar thing to be shocked about in the 1970s, but there you are. The floor was so practical for their wooden toys and their little ride-ons, and I was delighted with it.

With Barbara's help, and a bit more confidence in myself, I began to find my mothering feet and the courage to break a few rules, including no longer putting Colin before the children as much as I had. He was in Mustique a great deal of the time and I began to stay in England more with the children. As a result, we were all a great deal happier. I only wish I'd had the courage and confidence to do it sooner.

The mould of the traditional and rigidly old-fashioned nanny is fortunately well and truly broken now. I have no objection to a good nanny, though I know it's a very great luxury. I was delighted I had one, and I marvel at the many women these days who cope with childcare as well as working without any of the support staff that I enjoyed. I have absolutely no idea how they do it. But learning to get the balance right was key, and that took time and experience. I also think children benefit from having many people who love them in their lives, and from seeing their parents having a life beyond them, at least occasionally.

These days, fathers are much more involved in their children's lives than ours ever were. If mothers were distant, fathers were practically in different countries. It's a great benefit to children to see all that has changed. I often see dads out pushing prams or holding the hands of little ones on the way to the park. Wonderful. That would never have happened in my day.

The irony for me was that I learned the less Colin was involved, the easier I found it. In truth, Colin had never really grown up and wasn't particularly cut out to be a father. He loved having children but found it hard, partly because they took the attention away from him and his own wants and needs, and partly because he found the chaos of parenthood and young children hard to cope with.

Ideally, fathers are stable, reliable and mature. Colin didn't have any of those qualities. In fact, one of the real drawbacks for Charlie and Henry was how present Colin was in their lives when they were young before he moved more or less permanently abroad. He could have a very destabilising effect on them. One minute he was spoiling them terribly, exciting them with over-the-top games that had them squealing in a mixture of pleasure and terror, then the next he was losing his temper.

He was also not one of those fathers who wanted to let his children win. He always had to. Henry's sports day at prep school, which had been Colin's school too, was a calendar highlight for him. As a boy, he'd won the long jump there, and his athletic talent had been augmented in the army, so when he got to Sports Day, his main concern was which events he'd be allowed to compete in. He'd rush over to the masters to ask, 'What are the fathers allowed to do?' He couldn't wait to have his go. All the boys were standing around dreading the day, while Colin was champing at the bit to beat them hollow. He wasn't at all interested in what his son was doing. Actually, Henry was sitting next to me, eating strawberries and praying, like the rest of us, that Colin won whatever race he was competing in or else he'd be unbearable. Actually he quite often did win, thank goodness. But Colin was probably one of the few fathers there more interested in his own victory than his son's.

Our children loved him despite the difficulty of his unpredictability and tantrums. Barbara was usually very good at foreseeing trouble and sweeping the younger children out of the way, but occasionally she wasn't quick enough. At Glen once Amy was in the swimming pool and wouldn't get out when Barbara told her to. Colin and I were there with various guests, in all our finery for Sunday lunch, when he suddenly leaped into the pool, fully dressed, to pull her out. It gave her an awful fright. Another time, when May was three or four, she was sitting in his favourite chair and didn't get out the moment he told her to, so he picked her up and smacked her bottom. She just looked at him and said, 'Harder!' That made him collapse in fits of laughter, but one never knew which direction his temper would take. All the children had the wariness that anyone who spent time with Colin developed, the antennae always sensing when trouble was afoot.

On the other hand he offered enormous amounts of financial support to the older boys, and took us all on some remarkable journeys. On Mustique Charlie and Henry went to the village school and made lifelong friends there, and all of them loved the beaches and swimming. When Colin was living on St Lucia, he bought an elephant and I have a wonderful picture of him and the girls riding it. Colin also took us for some wonderful family holidays elsewhere. He decided we should go to a different European capital each year, which was like a Grand Tour for the children. On good days he was our own personal tour guide, sharing his knowledge and enthusiasm for art and architecture and spoiling us all rotten. But, of course, there were plenty of occasions too when he lost his temper and ruined the day. It must have been very confusing for the children when the attention, glamour and excitement of one moment turned into a terrible rage at the next.

He never liked overt shows of affection, or even to be touched very much, which made him rather cold and distant at times. He always seemed surprised when the children wanted to kiss him, as his own father had only ever given him handshakes.

I learned to make up for it as best I could by giving the children all the love and stability I could. I had to be the anti-Colin, to stay even-tempered, diplomatic and understanding, and always to be there when they needed me. That was so much easier to do with Christopher, May and Amy when I had more confidence in myself and as a mother, and when Colin was starting to go away for weeks on end. You would need to ask the children if I succeeded but I hope I did. I had learned by then how important it was to have times and places where we could all relax and recharge our batteries with simple pleasures and down-to-earth love in order to cope with the whirling dervish that was Colin. I passed that knowledge on to the younger children and I do hope it helped them. I hadn't yet learned those lessons in the crucial early years with Charlie and Henry.

Like so many parents, I felt that childhood sometimes seemed endless, and then – pouf – it was over. I wondered, where did it all go? I'm so happy I took a great many photographs so that I can remember the days when the children were so little and so sweet. Some of my happiest memories are of their parties, which I learned to love as much as any of our glamorous society events.

When I was a child, the craze for lavish birthday parties wasn't anything like it became. Although film stars' children in Hollywood might have been having circuses in the garden and rides on elephants, for us a cake in the nursery and a special tea was mostly what we got, and in wartime, even less. We were used to getting through with very little in the way of presents and so on. We were lucky, as my father was equerry to the King, to be invited to some wonderful Christmas parties at Buckingham Palace and Windsor Castle, where one was dazzled by the huge tree dressed in ornaments and candles, the thrill of the presents underneath and the delicious things to eat. At home, though, there was rarely a fuss made of us.

By the time I had my own children, ideas had changed. Perhaps we were determined to rebalance wartime privations by giving our children lots of what we had missed. My friends and I had lots of birthday parties for our children, and there were some splendid ones, especially when we moved to London. Those were the years when Charlie and Henry were at school and I was at home with Christopher and the twins while Colin was away focusing on the development of Mustique. My mother always said we spoiled all of our children, and perhaps we did, but we wanted them to have everything we'd missed out on, excitement, colour, parties and cake.

The children's birthday parties were such fun. We would book Smarty Arty, who was *the* children's entertainer of the day. He had a miniature gold coach that he would bring to parties and the birthday girl or boy was allowed to choose one friend, and only one, to go in the coach with them. It was then pulled around by a lady in a very unsuitable tight spangly outfit who took the part of the horse. She drew the coach around the garden and everyone clapped. Of course, it was clever of Smarty Arty only to allow two of the children on the coach, no matter how much the others begged. It made them all desperate for their turn, and the likelihood of him being booked for their parties went up accordingly. Smarty Arty also, very wisely, made sure there was sherry for the nannies, and later, as he got more successful, he suggested champagne, and they loved him even more. They could sit around, drinking and gossiping, while the children were entranced by the golden coach.

All the parties for my children and their friends followed the same plan: gathering in the afternoon to play, then have tea, then – nearly always – Smarty Arty. Besides the golden coach, he was also a very modest magician, so simple that you could see the tricks at once and unfortunately the children did as well: they sussed him out, and he would get quite crusty. So then we put on something for them to watch. There was no television to speak of, so we would put a wobbly old projector in front of a screen, and show a film or cartoon, which they all found very exciting.

Finally, the birthday cake would arrive. Supplied by a shop, it would be either a teddy bear or a doll for the girls, and a train or a car for the boys. It would be brought in, all lit up, to gasps of excitement, for the candles to be blown out. At the end, we always had to have party bags that, over the years, grew more and more elaborate. It started as just one little toy and some cake in a napkin to take away but before long our nanny Barbara told me that this wasn't enough. She would say, 'When we were at Lady So and So's party, there were lots of lovely presents in the party bag so I think we really need to put a little more into ours.'

'Of course, Barbara,' I'd say obediently. 'Whatever you think.'

For all my new-found confidence, and Barbara's fresh ideas, we were still aware of the traditions and norms that surrounded us, and wanted to keep up appearances. No one wanted to be shamed by the contents of a below-par party bag.

Children's birthday parties are meant to be sheer magic. Even today, my children remember Smarty Arty with joy, so he and his golden coach and those blessed party bags were worth every penny.

I've been lucky enough to go to the birthday parties of my grandchildren and great-grandchildren and watch the joy go on into the next generations. The formula and fashions may change a little – my granddaughters had parties at places called soft play, pits full of balls that I'm sure are covered with the most frightful germs – but parents go on marking their children's milestones, and I'm very glad they do.

Charlie was growing up to be extremely good-looking and was very sweet and funny. We hoped his difficulties were behind him. He hadn't managed to get into Eton, so went to Clifton College but that didn't suit him at all. Henry on the other hand had got into Eton and seemed to be thriving. Eventually, seeing how miserable Charlie was, we sent him to Frensham Heights, which was much less strict, but that turned out to be a terrible mistake. He was allowed to do whatever he wanted, and that turned out to mean taking a lot of drugs and not bathing. They drew the line at shop-lifting, which was what got him suspended.

Drugs were not a part of my world as they were not around when I was growing up. If they had been, perhaps I would not have been so innocent about what Charlie was getting up to and would have realised the dangers of his drug use much earlier. Finding out how destructive they could be was a terrible lesson for us all. Colin said that if he'd been exposed to cannabis and acid growing up, he could have seen himself going down the same hedonistic path as Charlie. Charlie was the child who was most like him in terms of temperament and showed the greatest signs of the kind of emotional difficulties that Colin suffered from, so perhaps he was right. It took us years to see how troubled Charlie was. He'd insist he was fine and we just accepted that and tolerated the emergence of his rituals as Charlie being Charlie. He had been smoking cannabis and taking LSD for some time, it appeared, and started taking heroin when he was in his mid-teens. We were so hopelessly innocent, we had no idea.

It was the most extraordinary time for young people in London. Going down the King's Road was like going to the theatre, there were so many eccentric-looking people. I remember Charlie telling me he was off shopping, and I asked where, and he said there was a wonderful shop called Granny Takes a Trip. I thought that sounded charming and asked if I should come and what sort of clothes did they have. And he said, 'Well, I don't think you'll be really interested, Mum.' It took me years to realise that Granny Takes A Trip could be a reference to drugs rather than a short holiday. Once we grasped what a hold drugs had taken on him, we did everything we could to help, but we were totally at sea.

In the late seventies, he went to New York and loved it there. He was friends with Robert Mapplethorpe and Andy Warhol, and seemed to feel this life of decadent glamour was his calling. He simply did not want to get clean at that stage. His drug dependence meant he could never find meaningful employment and however many times we sent him to rehab, nothing seemed to stick. He published and wrote for an underground magazine in London called the *Chelsea Scoop*, which included frank interviews with Andy Warhol, Quentin Crisp and Bianca Jagger among others, and showed how talented he was, but the drugs meant it was impossible for him to stick to it. We learned another painful lesson: that rehab would do nothing unless he wanted to quit. The decision to disinherit him was horrible, particularly given how much he had always loved Glen, but Colin and I agreed we had no choice. He was regularly stealing from us, and leaving lit cigarettes around Hill Lodge where we were at that time, and I was terrified he'd end up killing us all. The idea of Glen and its contents being sold to pay for heroin and room service, his preferred life at the time, was impossible. So, we put Glen into a family trust, though Colin agreed to support Charlie for the rest of his life and leave him his property in the West Indies.

I do worry about young people and drugs now, though at least they have the chance to know more about what they're getting into than Charlie did. In his last years, when he finally found the resolve to kick his habit, he took every opportunity to warn others about the dangers of addiction, which I think was very brave of him. The world seems to be full of drugs now, so easy to get hold of and so very hard to avoid. I imagine the social pressure to try them must be immense, and usually the people who most want them are the ones who really ought to avoid them. One young relative smoked cannabis for a while and, as a result, his character began to alter. I was highly relieved when he gave it up. I've never seen the appeal of feeling numbed or less aware of reality, and have never wanted anything to come between me and the natural high of a beautiful world. I know that's easy for me to say and I'm lucky not to have been tempted. Bitter experience has taught me, however, that drugs rarely make anyone life's easier or more enjoyable. There may be a few exceptions but generally they seem to cause more problems than they solve, and they certainly ravage one physically.

Henry was doing fine. He sailed through Eton. He had inherited Colin's and my love of travel and in 1979, at Machu Picchu in Peru, he met Tessa Cormack. They married on Mustique in 1983 after he graduated from Edinburgh University and we were absolutely delighted. By the time of the Peacock Ball for Colin's sixtieth birthday, however, Henry had announced he was gay and he and Tessa were amicably separated. They both came to the ball and Tessa was a tremendous help in organising all the fripperies for our costumes. Charlie was there too, using methadone now, and Christopher flew in to join us from his gap year. It was a wonderful occasion, but it marked a turning point. The physical toll Charlie's addiction was taking on him was clear, and I felt sure it would be only a matter of time before it killed him. Then, just before the ball, Colin told me Henry was HIV positive. I had to spend the party knowing that both my eldest boys were now living under a death sentence, while trying to be the good hostess I was trained and expected to be to our family and friends.

A few months later Christopher had his motorcycle accident and I couldn't believe I was destined to lose all three of my sons. He was brought back to England in a coma, and we were told there was no realistic hope of a recovery. I think it was then I learned what being a mother really means.

Depression for me was like darkness settling on my life and I had to find a way to make it through. I look back and wonder how I did. I have always had my Christian faith to support and nourish me, and I've found a great deal of solace in God, faith and prayers, but as I faced Henry's diagnosis, Christopher's accident and Charlie's latest relapse into heroin in quick succession, I started to pray properly. I had to have some very intense conversations with God in order to make sense of what was going on. He was taking my two eldest sons from me while I looked hopelessly on. I told Him He couldn't have Christopher too. If I dedicated myself to Christopher's recovery, refusing to give up on him for a second, then God would have to let me keep him.

Barbara, who had left us when the twins went away to school, came back to help me and we devoted ourselves to bringing Christopher out of his coma. I gave every ounce of my being to bringing him back. Barbara and I worked together, stimulating him for fifteen minutes every hour of every day. I cradled him like he was a baby again. Once he woke up, we had succeeded and we realised, with great joy, that he was still our lovely Christopher.

At first it was all about determination, simply getting on with the routine we had established. However, I quickly learned that if I was going to be of any use, just gritting my teeth and getting on with it wasn't going to be enough. Prayer and the prayers of others helped me through the dark early days, but after that joyous moment when Christopher opened his eyes and spoke to us, I realised that our journey was only beginning.

Life became so shrouded in darkness that I realised I had to make a conscious decision to reach for the light. If I was going to carry on, I had to treat myself with compassion and kindness. This was not only for my sake, but because I could not help others when I was deeply depressed. I had an enormous job to do. I had to bring Christopher back to the very best life he was capable of. I had to help my dying sons on their journeys, and support the others as well. The twins were only fifteen when Christopher had the accident, and only sixteen when Henry learned he was HIV positive. They still needed me. In order to be strong enough for everyone, I had to look after myself. What good would it do if I collapsed completely?

Not only that, but punishing myself would compound the feeling that somehow this was my fault. By being kind to myself, I was acknowledging that these awful events were not my fault. I had done my best. I was not to blame. When I faltered, and sometimes felt that I was guilty or had failed, I learned I could turn to friends who reminded me that I was not responsible, and that helped me cling to the idea that I didn't need to punish myself.

I sought out ways to feel better, building moments of peace, solitude and prayer into my life, if only for a few minutes a day. I had to give myself treats so that I felt cared for. These were very simple things. For example, I loved taking photographs and sticking them into my albums, so I would give myself the time, place and quiet to do that. I made an effort to see a film or go to an exhibition. Small things that would lift my spirits. I felt instinctively that I needed to do these things for myself. When I could, I turned to activities that would take me out of myself and allow me to forget the stress and sadness, if only for a short while. A trip to the opera could also offer a release; music was always an enormous source of healing. Activities like sailing, where I had to think only about what I was doing, stopped the terrible thoughts for a while and allowed me to recover enough to carry on. Sometimes I thought it would be easier just to collapse under it all, but that was not how I had been taught to behave as a child, and not what I had learned during my marriage. As Colin once said, we weren't brought up to throw in the towel, we were brought up to bite bullets and fold towels neatly. I had learned that to be able to do so I needed to take advantage of the refuges I had created, and grab every moment I could of solace and laughter with friends and family, so I put those lessons into practice. I also learned that it is possible to face unimaginable heartache and endless difficulties to do whatever you can to help your child, and that a mother's love is limitless.

As Christopher began to recover, I changed tack. Now, it was tough love. I wanted Christopher to recover from his disabilities to the greatest extent possible, so once he returned home, I didn't put anything into the house that would make life easier for him. No rails or hoists or lifts. I made him learn to walk, and climb the stairs even though it was agonising. I was so sure that it was the right thing that I stuck with it for his sake. I wanted him to regain his independence. He was only twenty and had, I hoped, a long life still to live. I needed to make sure he was able to look after himself as much as possible. It took five years of hard work and was worth every single second of struggle. He is, as he always was, a joy to be with. He has two lovely daughters with his first wife, and is now married to Johanna, who is such a help to us both.

With Christopher, Colin was different from the very beginning. For whatever reasons, probably to do with

Christopher's very affectionate nature, Colin was always wonderful with him and I was forever grateful that he never lost his temper with him.

Indeed Christopher could bring Colin's tantrums to a stop even when he was very little. Once when we were staying at Glen in the mid-seventies and Christopher was about five years old, Colin started screaming at me in the hallway, I can't remember why. I froze as I usually did. We had lots of lovely small pots of flowers in the hall and he started picking them up and throwing them at me. I was dodging as best I could when all of a sudden Christopher came running down the stairs, tore up to Colin and shouted, 'Stop it, Daddy! How dare you be so unkind to my mummy?'

I was desperately afraid for Christopher in that moment, but Colin simply burst out laughing, saying how wonderful it was that this tiny knight had come to my rescue. The next flowerpot stayed where it was and everything returned to normal.

After the accident, Colin was brilliant, and often helped Christopher in many ways, having him to live in St Lucia for a while to give me a rest and arranging for two local ladies to live nearby so that they could be on hand to help. He would take Christopher swimming all the time, which was one of the activities he really enjoyed and helped his fitness no end.

Once Colin told me that he was planning to go to Cuba and he was going to take Clarissa Eden, the Countess of

Avon, and Christopher with him. I thought it was a crazy idea. Christopher was severely disabled and needed a great deal of help all the time to do the simplest things and Clarissa could be rather grand and demanding. I envisaged the most terrible scenes, and Colin chewing carpets with rage every other hour.

When they got back, I asked Christopher if there had been many rows, certain I was about to hear of some epic meltdowns.

'Oh no,' Christopher said. 'None at all. Dad was brilliant. Absolutely amazing. Even when Clarissa didn't like her room, he was fine.'

Colin, it turned out, had planned everything to perfection from the start. As they were travelling with Clarissa, and she had been the wife of British prime minister Anthony Eden, they got very good treatment, with ambassadors to greet them, the best rooms possible, people on hand and cars laid on to help at all times. And, of course, I should have remembered that Colin never lost his temper in front of Clarissa and Christopher. If I'd only known how well he would behave, I would have gone too.

As Christopher was recovering, Henry was being greatly supported in his last years by his friend Kelvin O'Mard, who was an absolute angel and is still a very good friend of the family. He was at the Peacock Ball on Mustique, and at my ninetieth birthday party. Colin wasn't fazed when Henry came out, but watching poor Henry's rapid descent with HIV was hard for all of us, including Colin. When Henry bravely spoke out about his diagnosis, to help others, it went rather against Colin's wishes, and he found the press interest in Henry's life and death especially difficult to deal with, as I did. I'm very proud now that Henry made his HIV status public. It was important that he talked about his illness at a time when there was still so much terrible stigma attached. When I visited the Lighthouse hospice in London, I'd find myself talking to many young men whose parents refused to visit or acknowledge them. I'm so glad there was never any question of that in our family. Some of our friends avoided coming to stay with us, not because Henry was gay, but because HIV wasn't understood at the time and people found it all so frightening. But we had wonderful support from Princess Margaret, who would always come and stay, and Princess Diana who visited Henry and wrote to me afterwards.

Henry died early in the new year of 1990. It was a terrible loss for all of us and I couldn't believe he was really gone. Henry had taken a big interest in Buddhist spiritual practices so saying prayers for him with a Buddhist priest in India helped me a great deal, but the grief of losing a child is not something one ever gets over. You simply learn, if you're lucky enough, to live alongside it. Tessa took over the running of Glen, brought up their son Euan, and became a remarkable force in the world of green finance. She and Kelvin remained close friends until her far too early death in 2018. People still come up to me today to share happy memories of Henry. I'm so touched and grateful when that happens.

Charlie finally fought off his addiction, continuing to spend a lot of time at Glen where he met Sheilagh. They married in 1993. He wore a leopard-print velvet waistcoat and tartan trews. Sheilagh wore a white lace dress and veil and looked beautiful. That night we danced reels and let our hair down. They had Cody the following year. It was wonderful to see them so happy and they were terribly in love, but our fear that his addictions had ruined his health were justified. Charlie was diagnosed with hepatitis C while Cody was still a toddler. None of us were quite sure how serious it was, and Sheilagh and Charlie reassured us they expected a rough few months, but no immediate danger. Unfortunately the disease took him very quickly. Colin was in the West Indies when Charlie died, and I was on holiday in Morocco. The grief was almost overwhelming.

I felt the whisper of censorious judgements over Charlie and Henry's deaths from drugs and AIDS (a source of great pain in itself as I felt they were saying my boys had brought it on themselves and so somehow it was less painful). I could hardly comprehend I had lost both of my eldest boys. My friends were wonderful and offered comfort and sympathy. I could not have managed without them. Charlie's funeral, with the press hammering on the doors of the church and trying to get their story about the Tennant Curse, was a terrible, terrible day. I'm so glad he had those final years of happiness, but burying a second son was almost too much for me. I knew, though, that I needed to be strong for Colin and my surviving children, and the partners and children of those I had lost.

Forgiveness is a central message in the Christian faith and, while it is far from easy, I have learned it plays a huge part in getting through the pain and starting to heal.

When Christopher had his accident, I had to forgive him for ignoring my advice not to get on a motorbike. He had not worn a helmet. He was riding pillion at night and they didn't see the roadworks they hit. More than that, I had to forgive the other boy involved who was driving the bike and only broke his shoulder. Christopher almost died and was permanently disabled. I felt so desperately angry that these banal circumstances were the reason the accident had happened, and furious that the other boy had suffered so little. Then I realised I couldn't help Christopher properly if I didn't forgive the other boy. I needed to get rid of the anger inside me if I was going to nurse him properly. So, I took the very conscious decision to do so. I told myself that it could easily have been the other way around, and that no one was to blame. Anger is easy and forgiveness is not. It took all my strength and determination to get there, propelled by my faith. Once I made that effort, I found I was so much freer to concentrate on helping my son recover.

Sometimes one needs to forgive the dead for dying. After Henry died, I felt a rush of rage at him for being so careless and catching HIV when I had told him to take precautions. I was desperately angry with Charlie for becoming addicted to drugs and dying of hepatitis just when he was happily married and a father, with his troubles behind him.

The support of my friends and the consolation of faith helped me to let go of this anger, forgive my boys for leaving us, and concentrate on the love I felt for them and the happiness they had brought me.

When you are going through something, you focus on that day or that hour. Only afterwards, sometime when you've recovered or healed, do you begin to understand the extent of what happened. There were times when I felt close to rock bottom, engulfed by grief and heartbreak, so I hope sharing what I have learned can be helpful to others. The pain is always with me and will never go but I've learned to live with it, and I think it's made me stronger. Once you've been through dark times, nothing ever seems as bad again. I think that's one of the reasons why I treasure every day now. I learned to forgive myself and others. I learned to take care of myself, that the worst can be endured and that things can and do get brighter again in the end. I've also learned that dwelling on the end of their lives or the fact they are not here any more will not help them or me, but remembering and celebrating them can be joyous. I want their children and grandchildren to know that Charlie and Henry were loved, and how much joy they brought me. So when I feel the deep sadness of their loss threatening to overwhelm me, I concentrate on that instead.

Things have changed indeed since Charlie was born. I always considered myself much more involved with the children than many of my friends were with theirs, but I realise that's still a world away from many parents' experience now. I do love the fact that families are all so different these days. I recently met a lovely gay couple who have a house near me in Norfolk and they said, 'We don't give dinner parties these days because of our two children.'

'Have you adopted?' I asked, interested.

'Oh, no,' they said. 'They're ours with a surrogate mother, and we each gave sperm for one of the children.'

Well, goodness! That was quite unknown when I was young. Women can have children without men, and vice versa. Medical advances and cultural changes have completely altered the landscape of families. As long as children are loved, wanted and cared for, then as far as I'm concerned it all adds to the happiness and diversity of life.

I see in my grandchildren the challenges that modern parents face. We live in a much more uncertain world. The pressures of social media are influencing children in ways we very often can't control, and there seems to be a great deal of confusion about the effects these huge technological changes will have on how we communicate with each other and so much else besides. I do worry for our young men and women, but they have my sympathy, as do the parents who are trying to guide their children through these murky new waters and out to happiness and stability in whatever form they take. What I have learned, more than anything else, is that the agony and uncertainty of motherhood is worth it, and being a mother is to discover an infinite reservoir of love and resolve in one's heart.

CHAPTER SIX

Lady in Waiting

I WAS DELIGHTED when Princess Margaret asked me to be one of her ladies in waiting after Amy and May were born. The offer came at just the right time. With Barbara to look after the children and Colin away more and more, it was wonderful to find a new role that suited me so well. It reinforced the idea that I was a person of value in my own right, rather than simply being Colin's wife. It really was the beginning of a new chapter in my life, and some fifteen years later, when I was going through my darkest times, Princess Margaret's friendship and practical good sense were an enormous support and comfort.

Like being a wife or a mother, the role of lady in waiting didn't come with a job description or any training. I had to learn as I went along. I was lucky, though, as my mother could give me some idea about what was involved as she was lady of the bedchamber to our late Queen. Princess Margaret reminded me of her in many ways. They were both brave and no-nonsense, and didn't believe in dwelling on life's difficulties. The early training my mother gave me about behaving correctly in public, not complaining and putting others first was also particularly useful, and life with Colin had already taught me to be adaptable.

I discovered I enjoyed the work very much. It was a pleasure to be useful, both to Princess Margaret, and to the Royal Household in general. Accompanying the Princess on her official duties gave me a great insight into all of the valuable work the Royal Family does and, of course, the role gave me opportunities for all sorts of adventures I wouldn't have had otherwise.

Our activities were recorded in the Court Circular, the official record of the engagements of the Royal Family, which is still published every day. It has a very formal style, and is organised by the Royal Household, so Princess Margaret's engagements were always listed under Kensington Palace. A typical entry would be something like 'The Princess Margaret, Countess of Snowdon, undertook engagements today in Southampton' or wherever it was, or 'was present at such and such an event' for film premieres, concerts or dinners. These were almost always given in aid of one or other of the many charities she was involved with. A lot of openings were involved, too, from reservoirs to visitors' centres, and the occasional launching of a boat. Ladies in waiting were always noted as being 'in attendance'.

Looking back I was in attendance quite a lot and at all sorts of things. One of my duties was also to represent

Princess Margaret at events she couldn't attend herself. The Royal Family very rarely go to funerals, so you'll often see in the Court Circular various members being represented by equerries or ladies in waiting like myself. After Princess Margaret died, I occasionally performed the same role for the then Prince Charles and Duchess of Cornwall. It was always an honour to do so and I enjoy popping up in the Court Circular again from time to time.

The visits to towns and cities around the United Kingdom with Princess Margaret reminded me of trips I used to make with the House of Citizenship, and in the same way they meant I had the chance to meet and learn about all manner of people, industries, charities and places I would never have done otherwise and which I often found fascinating. Foreign trips often involved us seeing sights and ceremonies one wouldn't get to experience as an ordinary traveller, as well as staying in very grand embassies, which was always fun. These goodwill visits were arranged by the Foreign Office, and we were carefully briefed on who was who, and what topics were safe to discuss and which were best avoided. The schedules were always packed, and rigidly organised weeks in advance. State dinners at Buckingham Palace for visiting dignitaries were splendid occasions, and I went to quite a few over the years. It is always marvellous seeing the Palace at its best, with the table laid for a hundred and fifty people each with a dozen pieces of cutlery in silver gilt and an array of glasses perfectly arranged. The staff made it all look effortless, though these occasions can take a year to plan.

Being a lady in waiting was not unlike being Colin's wife in some ways with the amount of behind-the-scenes troubleshooting it involved. While other members of Princess Margaret's household organised the practical details of getting us from one event to another, my job was often to serve as a buffer between her and other people. Sometimes that meant answering the questions and queries of those who didn't want or didn't have the chance to approach her directly. For example, people would often want to know what colour outfit she'd be wearing, so they could choose flowers to go with it, or they wanted to make sure someone else wasn't wearing the same. At receptions I'd often be in charge of making sure that she spoke to everybody she needed to, or wasn't monopolised by someone overbearing. I could swoop in and whisk her away without her having to appear rude. I learned to watch for any sign she was becoming uncomfortable or bored and did my best to intervene.

I also learned that if at all possible it was a good idea to try to make sure her hosts knew some of her likes and dislikes in advance. They might seem small things, but they often helped to make a visit go smoothly and ensured everyone got the most out of an occasion. She liked to light her own cigarettes and people were always falling over themselves to light them for her, then looked terribly upset when she waved them away, something that could be avoided by simply telling people in advance not to try. She drank gin and tonic at lunchtime and whisky and water in the evening, so I would always check that someone had an eye on her glass to see if she needed another. She often did!

When Princess Margaret was being introduced to large groups of people, each individual often had only the briefest moment with her. We met men and women who had done huge amounts for their communities at these occasions and I understood meeting the Princess was often a great occasion for them, but it could feel terribly fleeting. I would hang back and have a quick chat with as many of them as possible. Though talking to me was never going to be as exciting as meeting Princess Margaret, I hope that a conversation with someone else from the household prolonged the moment for them a bit. I often found that someone would have planned something they particularly wanted to say, but meeting the Princess could be rather overwhelming so before they'd had a chance to get it out, she would have been swept off. Time-keeping had to be terribly strict to keep us on schedule. I could pause and chat, and they got to say to me whatever remark or pleasantry they had been planning when they were much less nervous. I could assure them I'd pass it on. I think the Queen Consort does something similar for King Charles, as people are rather tongue-tied when they meet him, and find it easier to talk to her. He calls her his eyes and ears.

Over my first few years as lady in waiting, I learned which problems and questions were likely to come up and how to prepare for them. That made my job much easier over the many years to come.

There was always the challenge of the unexpected, though. Princess Margaret had her own security men, but I was always aware of people photographing her and I worried about strangers, who could have been anyone, getting dangerously close to her in crowds. Once in Australia, I did grab a man who reached for her. He was there before any of the security and detectives could do a thing, and I pushed him away. I did it without thinking, but it made me wonder what I might have done if I had ever been in a position to sacrifice my life for her, leaping in front of a man with a gun or a knife, for instance. Anything was possible and, of course, I was lady in waiting at the chilling moment when Lord Mountbatten was assassinated by the IRA; in 1974 a man had tried to kidnap Princess Anne on the Mall, shooting and injuring her bodyguard and chauffeur in the process. I assume I would have done what I could to protect Princess Margaret without even thinking, just as I did in Australia. I'm just terribly glad it wasn't required, though I do believe I'd had enough training to think quickly in a crisis.

Some of the Royal Family still have ladies in waiting in the old-fashioned way. The Queen always had them and so does Princess Anne but the younger royals have a more professional team to look after them nowadays, as do King Charles and the Queen Consort. Given the very different challenges they face in the age of twenty-four-hour news, social media and so on, that's probably a good idea. Naturally mistakes are still made, and the royals often have to carry the can for decisions they had no part in.

Ladies in waiting didn't receive payment, but as Princess Margaret's visits were often made at the request of the government we were given a clothes allowance. The allowances weren't huge, as I remember, but enough for a couple of suitable dresses and an occasional hat. Being on show all the time meant that Princess Margaret normally travelled with a hairdresser who I was allowed to share when we were on tour. It was so enjoyable to be made to look glamorous every day.

When I was living with Princess Margaret in Kensington Palace while my London flat was being refurbished, my London hairdresser Simon came there to do my hair for me. The Princess came in one day to say hello, and said to him, 'I'm so glad to meet you, as there's something I'd like to mention. Lady Glenconner has a very noble brow and I think you should show it more.'

When she'd gone, he fell about laughing. 'What about your noble brow!' he said.

He never let me forget it. I still have no idea what she wanted him to do to me, and neither did he.

I had to keep a semi-royal wardrobe of my own to attend events with Princess Margaret, so I had a great selection of silk dresses, hats, smart shoes, gloves and handbags. Evening occasions meant long dresses, high heels (not too high, of course: I didn't want to tower over Princess Margaret or, worse, fall over), and smart embroidered evening bags. Travelling with enough clothes for all occasions meant I had to become an expert packer and planner. My mother took her maid when she was travelling with the Queen, but I normally relied on one of the housemaids of the government residences where we usually stayed when abroad. They were very good and I'm so glad they were as we'd often have to change four times a day for different events, and often pretty quickly, given the packed schedules. One's clothes could get into complete disarray without their help.

Princess Margaret normally travelled with her maid, too, but that wasn't always the case, particularly on Mustique. I remember once having a terrible time trying to pack for her. She always wore boned corsets, and even boned swimming costumes. She had got into the habit of wearing them in the fifties when the boned look from Dior was all the rage, and wore them for the rest of her life. I warned her they might be uncomfortable on Mustique, given how hot it was, but she said they gave her confidence and I couldn't argue with that. Anyway, she told me these boned swimming costumes were supposed to sit in a special tray in one of her cases, but I could not for the life of me get them to lie flat long enough for me to be able to shut the lid. They simply sprang up and jumped out of the case as if they had a life of their own.

I realised for someone as inexperienced with these garments as I was, this was going to be a two-person job.

'Ma'am, would you come here? I'm trying to pack for you but your bathing suits keep popping out.'

She joined me and we tried again and again with her holding them flat while I tried to snap the case shut on them. They were like wild beasts.

'One, two three,' we'd count, and I tried to slam the case shut but we kept missing the crucial moment and the awful things just flew out again. Before long we were both help-less with laughter, which didn't help. I have no idea how her maid managed them so effortlessly, but that was a skill I never learned.

Princess Margaret particularly loved jewellery. She didn't have a huge amount but she chose carefully. The diamond tiara she wore at her wedding became quite famous and indelibly associated with her. She bought it herself, as she didn't have one of her own. Patrick Plunket, who had such good taste and was once a trustee of the Wallace Collection, saw it for sale at auction and told her about it. It was called the Poltimore tiara, made for Lady Poltimore by Garrards in the nineteenth century in ornate Victorian style with lots of floral scrolling and ornaments. It was also very high, which suited the fashion of the 1960s as Princess Margaret could pile up her hair inside it. She looked dazzling in it. Her husband Tony later took a famous photograph of her wearing it in the bath, with an expression that was both happy and rather coquettish. She bought the tiara for £5,500 and it was sold for nearly £1 million after her death. No one knows who bought it. I wonder where it is now.

Princess Margaret loved building her jewellery collection. If she broke a bottle over the prow of a ship, she would quite often be given a piece of jewellery, sometimes diamonds if she was very lucky. If the setting wasn't quite to her taste, she would take it to her jeweller's to be made up into something she really liked. Naturally she wouldn't do that with important gifts, such as the beautiful diamond necklaces her parents had given her, or with regimental brooches, but anything that wouldn't be seen again in an official capacity could be changed. I remember seeing sketches by the jeweller Theo Fennell on her desk for some lovely brooches she'd asked him to design. She enjoyed commissioning interesting things to be made, sometimes designing them herself. I particularly remember a coral and diamond necklace she had made. She loved swimming but never went snorkelling, so she had it made as she imagined coral to be, rather than what it actually looked like, but it was very pretty.

Princess Margaret could be generous in giving away her things when they were no longer needed but she and I were not the same size: she was smaller than me and much bustier, so her clothes would never have fitted. She did, though, give me the occasional handbag. It was always lovely to have a present from her. After she died, all her possessions were auctioned in a sale, but before that happened, the ladies in waiting were allowed to choose one or two things, such as costume jewellery or clothes, as a memento. I chose a coat and dress that she wore for the Queen Mother's hundredth birthday, and the earrings she was wearing in a photograph taken by Lord Lichfield in Mustique, my favourite photo of her, in a straw hat on a chaise longue.

There were some other lovely perks to being a lady in waiting as well as the travel and the people we met. We received tickets for Wimbledon and Ascot, which was always great fun. I am also still part of the NHS practice, which is based in the stables at Buckingham Palace and looks after everyone in the Royal Household, including the staff. I don't have to go often as fortunately I am quite healthy, but it certainly makes getting one's flu jab more of an occasion.

For all the glamour and fun, it has to be admitted that a lot of the work the Royal Family does is rather dull. I never had to go to half as many things as Princess Margaret, but even then they could all rather blur into one another after a while. The royals are very good, I think, at looking enthused about everything they are shown and spending hours shaking hands with one group of strangers after another, but no matter the variety of places and people they meet, it can get a bit repetitive. There's a common misconception that royals can do whatever they please, and behave however they want. Of course that's not true. Their schedules are carefully organised so that they can be as useful as possible to the government and to the various charitable causes they support, and they have to be incredibly scrupulous and make sure to be perfectly behaved at all times. If they behave beautifully, no one notices, but if they put a foot out of line, they jolly well get a reputation for being rude and difficult. At the same time everyone is ready to take a photograph and if they look distracted or unhappy for even a second at an event, someone will publish a photograph of that moment and write a silly or hurtful story underneath it.

I honestly don't know how they manage it. Even with the training I received in good manners and behaving well in public, I still found it difficult to maintain the right expression for hours at some ceremony or other, no matter the weather or my personal circumstances that day. I'm so glad I have never had to live my life on display to the degree the Royal Family do. There was the terrible attention we received when Henry and Charlie died, but that didn't last for a lifetime, and I do sometimes get recognised on the street now, but that normally just results in a lovely chat with someone who has read and enjoyed one of my books. I've certainly never been pursued by the paparazzi and the press, day in and day out, the way the Royal Family are.

Mobile phones with cameras mean they have even less opportunity for any privacy now. I was giving a lunch for the then Duchess of Cornwall and her sister not so long ago, in a small restaurant where we thought we were fairly private, and suddenly the Duchess flinched. I realised the woman on the next table had her phone out, possibly about to take a photograph. I don't think she did, but it was telling that the Duchess is clearly on her guard and is very used to being photographed even when she is off duty, trying to have a little time to herself and an ordinary outing with friends. In the old days, you could often spot a photographer trying to take a surreptitious photograph because of the huge camera and the long lens. They needed time to focus too before they clicked, so one usually had a chance to prepare or dodge. Now it's all very quick and easy, and everyone is a potential press photographer, but we all need a chance to relax and drop our guard from time to time.

The fact that everyone has a camera on their phone has changed regular royal engagements too. The working members of the Royal Family often find themselves facing a sea of phones instead of faces, which does seem a shame.

I'm glad my mother taught me to keep my feet on the ground. It means I haven't always lived in a bubble of privilege and wealth and that's been very good for me. It's very hard for any member of the Royal Family to have that experience. Everybody around them treats them with great deference and it is up to them to remember that they are still only human when people are rolling out red carpets, laughing uproariously at their every joke, and agreeing with every word they say with awe and wonder, not to mention polishing and cleaning everything in sight before they lay their eyes on it. The Queen always understood that the deference paid to her was because of her position and what she represented, not because of who she was as a person. I think one of the reasons she was so loved was because she was not arrogant or haughty.

I grew up being quite used to meeting members of the Royal Family. I'm always respectful, but the mysterious quality of royalty was something I was used to long before I became a lady in waiting. It was fascinating and rather humbling to see how strongly that quality can affect people who aren't used to such encounters. In Princess Margaret's presence, people occasionally stuttered, fell over (more than one lady sank so low in her curtsey that she collapsed), fainted or turned oddly deaf.

Looking back I think life must have been very strange for Princess Margaret. She was brought up in a very grand way and was always very well looked after, but everything changed when Edward VIII abdicated. She had been part of a close family of four, until suddenly their status altered dramatically and in different degrees. Her father became King and Emperor at a time when half the world was coloured pink on a map, her mother became Queen, her sister was now heir to the throne and was plunged into being prepared to take over that great office.

Princess Margaret was suddenly out on a limb. She was a clever and curious woman, but didn't have the chance to have a formal education. She was a true friend, but those friendships were almost always coloured by her status. She was a performer, and loved to entertain, but she was only allowed to play one role, that of princess, and the press made her the 'difficult' sister. Every story needs heroes and villains, as I now know from writing my novels. With her sister as the future Queen, the press needed a 'bad' princess and Margaret was the only available candidate. The fact she enjoyed the company of creative people, a cigarette and a drink made it easy to cast her as a rebel to be celebrated or judged. Mostly judged. Sometimes it seemed as though her life was either a chorus of riotous cheers, or outraged boos, without much in between.

Even on Mustique and at Glen, poor Princess Margaret wasn't always safe from prying and judgemental eyes. Colin made sure the press were kept off the island, and Glen was a private estate, so the house was out of reach of long lenses, but we all had cameras too. I made every effort to protect her, but having a close friend who is also royalty could create temptations even in my own family. I am sorry to say Charlie sold some private pictures of Princess Margaret, taken at Glen, when she was dressed up as Mae West. She was immensely forgiving, knowing that the temptation to make some money quickly was overpowering when he was in the grip of heroin addiction. It was very kind of her. I sued, asserting my right to the photographs, which meant that they could never be published, and won. I gave half of the damages awarded to Erin Pizzey and bought myself a nice piece of jewellery with the rest. I learned Princess Margaret particularly valued friends who didn't want anything from her and who weren't so overwhelmed by her royal status that they couldn't act normally. Most of the time she was kind, generous and patient, as well as tremendously brave, but, of course, at times she got a little grumpy when she felt she was being pushed around. Sometimes I couldn't help blaming other people for bringing out the worst in her.

She understood that people wanted to see her and that she could bring a great deal of excitement and pleasure simply with her presence, but she was not a performing doll to be taken out on demand, and I learned that what she disliked most was having surprises sprung on her.

We were staying with a friend in New York who had arranged for us to go to the theatre. Just as we were about to leave, she stopped Princess Margaret, saying, 'Ma'am, the cast is so looking forward to meeting you afterwards.'

This was exactly what she didn't like.

'I don't want to meet them,' she said, 'and I'm not going to.'

Our friend was mortified and begged me to ask her to change her mind. In an effort to please everyone, I had a little private chat with her and said, 'Ma'am, you really can't disappoint them. It would be such a shame. I know you should have been asked if you would mind, but it's a little too late now . . .'

'Anne,' she said, irritated, 'why don't people just ask me? Why do they spring it on me like this?'

'They think you'll say no, I expect.'

'Well, I will say no if they don't.'

'Perhaps you could just this once? After all, it's so lovely for us to be taken to the theatre.'

'Are you bullying me, Anne?'

'Perhaps just a little, ma'am.'

'Oh, all right, then. As you've forced me.'

Then she was charm itself, but of course she liked to be consulted.

It was the same if Princess Margaret was staying somewhere. When she was at a private house with friends, she didn't want to be on duty, yet so often, when she visited, many of them would roll out a few bishops and chiefs of police as though these were the people she absolutely longed to spend her spare time with. She was expected to accept this, though it meant she was essentially being asked to work in her time off. She hated finding she was being asked to perform her royal role or that she was on display without warning. It happened so often she tended to be rather suspicious, and if she suspected anything was afoot she could be guilty of rudeness. Once, when she heard that her hostess was paying back all her local friends and dignitaries by inviting dozens of them to dinner with her, she really did refuse to go. The hostess called me in floods, begging me to change Princess Margaret's mind, but I couldn't. Princess Margaret simply felt used, and not welcomed for her own sake. She wouldn't back down, to the hostess's huge embarrassment. But she thought she'd been asked along for a pleasant evening with friends rather than to a charity or public event, so I think she had the right to feel a bit miffed.

When Princess Margaret was invited somewhere, I always hoped her hosts would ring up and ask what she would actually enjoy eating. I was naturally always happy to explain. So often they simply assumed what a royal princess must like and subjected her to huge meals of very rich food instead of the quite simple fare she preferred. She became very cunning at covering up food on her plate so no one could see that she hadn't eaten all of it, managing to avoid offending anyone – a skill that proved very useful when we were often served some rather alarming food abroad. What Princess Margaret really liked was good plain nursery food: shepherd's pie, scrambled eggs, poached fish, mashed potato and so on. When she was going to a private home, the very last thing she wanted was yet another six-course banquet.

The key to a happy occasion was to treat Princess Margaret with consideration, as any guest would reasonably expect. When she came to Norfolk, I made sure in advance that she liked anything I'd planned. If I invited anyone else, it would only be those who would enrich her stay and increase her enjoyment, and I would always make sure she had agreed to whatever visitor I'd suggested. We ate simple food and enjoyed simple pleasures. As a result she was always wonderful company and I'm delighted my farm-house became a refuge for her as well as for me in difficult times. I'm sorry she offended some people, but they made such sweeping assumptions about how a princess should be treated, rather than thinking of her as a person with quite·ordinary likes and dislikes. She needed a rest from the usual round of royal duties, not to have her hosts force her into continuing with them in private.

It's not surprising she liked to assert her own free will occasionally, though once it terrified the life out of me. We were on a trip to see the Angel Falls in Venezuela. It's the world's largest uninterrupted waterfall, dropping for thousands of feet over the edge of a mountain in the Canaima National Park. We went there with friends, flying into the local airport and then travelling by Land Rover through the jungle to the river, where a huge lunch table had been laid on the bank. It was obviously a marvellous treat, to which we were all looking forward very much. The object of the trip was to fly up and see the amazing view of the Falls from above as they plummeted down the mountain, but when we arrived, one of the security men went up to Nigel Napier, Princess Margaret's private secretary, and said, 'Princess Margaret cannot fly in this plane. It's not safe. We've checked it and absolutely not.'

Nigel then told me, and I had the job of letting Princess Margaret know. 'I'm terribly sorry, ma'am, I know it's very disappointing but we can't go up. The aeroplane isn't safe, apparently.'

Princess Margaret was indeed disappointed, but seemed to accept it and we started having drinks before lunch. After a while, I said to Nigel, 'Have you seen Princess Margaret? Where is she? She was here a minute ago.'

We looked about and there was no sign of her, when suddenly there was a huge roar and up went the plane with Princess Margaret in it. She had sneaked away without telling us.

We watched in horror, our hearts in our mouths, as the little aircraft buzzed around above the mountain. I'm sure Princess Margaret was having a ball, whizzing about and looking at the Falls, but we were ill with worry the entire time.

'If anything happens,' Nigel said, white-faced, 'we'll be blamed. We're in charge.'

I knew he was right but what could we do now she was actually up in the air? To our great relief, she landed safely. When she rejoined us, Nigel was visibly angry and so was

I, although I didn't show it as much. He said very sternly, 'Ma'am, you shouldn't have done that! You put us in an impossible position. We're responsible for you.'

'We were so worried, ma'am. It was dreadful!' I added.

She looked very abashed and said, 'Am I getting a ticking off?'

'Yes, you are, ma'am,' I said.

'But it was all fine,' she said stubbornly.

Two days later, the plane crashed and was completely destroyed. She was incredibly lucky and I still feel slightly sick when I think about it.

Usually the flying was the least stressful bit of going abroad with Princess Margaret. If we were going on a state tour, we were sometimes able to use the Queen's Flight, which was a great pleasure and privilege. We handed over our passports at the beginning of the journey and didn't see them again till we got back. Our luggage was whisked away and we didn't have to worry about airports or queues or security. We were driven right up to the plane so we could just get out and climb the steps. It was all very pleasant and smooth.

Most of the time we flew on commercial flights, and it wasn't quite such a breeze, although Princess Margaret was always in first class and I went with her, so still rather luxurious. In America we had to go through security machines on arrival. They detected metal and Princess Margaret had steel-boned corsets on.

'I'm going to go off like a firework, Anne!' she said crossly.

She had to go through, though, like everyone else, and she did cause rather a lot of beeping. Meanwhile, with the distraction going on, her security officer simply walked around the machine instead of going through, and that way he kept his gun on him, instead of giving it in, which he was strictly supposed to do. So Princess Margaret's corset worked in her favour that day, even though she was so cross about the machine.

Once, travelling with Princess Margaret, I found myself in the unusual position of having to persuade Americans to give up their guns, which was a great test for my diplomatic skills. When we were in the British Virgin Islands, staying at the High Commission, an important American official was invited for a formal dinner. There was a bit of fuss when it was realised that he would be bringing armed security guards, because the British contingent couldn't allow armed men into the presence of a member of the Royal Family. They came to me to smooth out the situation.

When the VIP arrived with his phalanx of guards, I explained the rule that no one is allowed to carry a weapon in the presence of a member of the Royal Family unless it is their own security. A very sensible one, I think. At first the official was indignant and said he wouldn't come into the dinner at all in that case. But after I'd done a bit of soft-soaping, telling him how desperately Princess Margaret wanted to meet him, he eventually agreed that his guards would leave their guns in the hall, rather like umbrellas or hats. The diplomatic issue and the breach of the Princess's security was, thankfully, averted and the dinner went ahead.

The people Princess Margaret treated worst were probably those who were most desperate to ingratiate themselves with her, and sometimes I just couldn't make her see that she was not behaving well to them. One of these was our friend Drue Heinz, a British-born American philanthropist and patron of the arts. Drue was lovely, kind and generous, but she was so eager to please that Princess Margaret became a little complacent.

One year, for some mysterious reason, Drue gave Princess Margaret a very expensive fountain, the sort that goes on a wall, with a gargoyle that spouted water into a basin.

She rang up one day, anxious, to ask if it had arrived.

I said, 'Yes, it has. I saw it in a huge box in the garden.'

'I haven't heard anything.'

'I'm sure you will. Princess Margaret is thrilled with it.'

'I'd love to come and see it,' Drue said wistfully.

'Of course you must come.'

Then I reminded Princess Margaret to ring Drue and thank her. 'She wants to come and see it. Is it up?'

'Oh, it's so tiresome,' she said. 'I have no idea where to put it . . . I'll decide soon.'

Well, she didn't decide. This went on for some time, with Drue ringing up and me putting her off until Drue said, almost in tears, 'Has she thrown it away?'

'No, no, no, I promise she hasn't.'

It was now almost time for the Chelsea Flower Show, which Drue was invited to as one of Princess Margaret's guests, to thank her for all her kindness. This was the ideal moment to view the fountain. When Drue arrived at Kensington Palace, we finally went to see the blessed thing, setting off through the garden with her. It was a big garden and we went all the way to the end of it until we reached the very back, where Princess Margaret began to push her way through enormous bushes. Poor Drue, all dressed up for the flower show, had to fight her way through leaves and branches. Princess Margaret had very naughtily placed the fountain on a wall at the back, where it was completely invisible.

'Oh, ma'am,' said Drue, dismayed. 'No one can see it!'

'I can,' said Princess Margaret. 'I often go through the bushes and there it is.'

Drue had to accept this unlikely claim but I did feel it wasn't really good enough.

Afterwards I did my best to reassure Drue: 'She really does love the fountain. And that place is her secret spot for when she's feeling down.'

It was a completely bogus story but it made Princess Margaret seem a little less rude.

I learned to do quite a lot of this diplomacy, being clear and trying to be reasonable if I thought Princess Margaret was doing the wrong thing, helping to pacify her when she felt upset, or smooth ruffled feathers of friends or visitors who felt they'd been mistreated. I used the same methods of gentle persuasion I'd learned with Colin. Life with him had also taught me to pick my battles carefully, and not get worked up.

That proved very useful as we often had to negotiate quite delicate situations in all sorts of varied circumstances. Princess Margaret had a mind of her own and, like Colin, was a strong personality, which meant a delicate approach was often necessary. Sometimes she would concede, and sometimes not, but she could usually see exactly what I was doing and would say, 'You win this time, Anne.' Instead of shouting and storming at me the way Colin did, she sometimes took revenge on me in small, harmless ways, such as making me laugh till I cried at entirely inappropriate moments, or when she once told someone I'd love to hold a koala, when I really didn't want to at all. She was very amused when it weed over me. I saw the funny side of that occasion too, once the koala had been removed. We laughed a great deal. It lightened the strain of all those engagements and careful negotiations. If anything ridiculous happened, we always knew we'd be able to make it into a good story afterwards.

Not all our outings together were official. Princess Margaret absolutely loved Scottish dancing, which she'd learned at Balmoral, and later we went to the Caledonian Ball in London on a few occasions. She always looked wonderful in a silk dress and the Royal Stuart tartan worn as a sash pinned at the shoulder with a big brooch. All of the Royal Family reel and seem to enjoy it hugely, especially the Queen, who would always smile broadly throughout. The Queen Mother moved very gracefully and slowly, and all royal reels were a little more sedate than the energetic whooping, stomping and clapping in the Highlands. Dancing was a chance for them to let their hair down a little and relax, and the Ghillies Ball at Balmoral was a time when the family and the staff danced together, which they all enjoyed.

Not all of our outings were glamorous. When I was living with Princess Margaret at Kensington Palace we used to go to the Coronet cinema in Notting Hill. In those days you could smoke in cinemas but only on the top tier, so we'd go to the upper balcony and sit there, where it was terribly dirty and very smelly.

'Ma'am, it really is too disgusting up here!' I'd say.

'Oh, Anne, you're so fussy. It doesn't matter, as long as I can smoke.'

We went there quite often, sitting with all the other smokers puffing away. Sometimes it was so thick with smoke, I could hardly see the film. Thanks to my mother and Princess Margaret, I'm quite sure I've breathed in the equivalent of hundreds of packets of cigarettes during my life but, so far, with no ill effects. I don't think the other cinema-goers even noticed the Princess was there, hidden as she was in clouds of smoke. And if they did, they probably thought she just looked like Princess Margaret as they simply didn't expect to see her there. That quite often happened when we were out: you would see people do a double-take, then shake their heads and continue on their way. Those visits to the cinema were not recorded in the Court Circular.

Fortunately for Princess Margaret, smoking didn't take too much of a toll on her looks until her final years. The Queen and Princess Margaret always had the most beautiful complexions. The Queen, though, never went in the sun, unless she was abroad, and certainly not without a hat. She always went to Scotland for her summer holidays, which was also a very good way of preventing sun damage. Princess Margaret loved the sun and liked to be tanned, but she never wanted a tan on her face. She stopped that by insisting on our wearing full makeup all the time, even when we went swimming. 'Put on lots of makeup, Anne, proper foundation and powder. It's good for the skin,' she would say. 'Much better than some greasy sun cream.' It certainly worked in her case.

She made smoking look very elegant, with her cigarette in a long holder, but elegant as she made it look, smoking was a terrible habit, and she had to give up eventually, which she did without any fuss. She pretended it was no effort, but I'm sure it was much harder than she admitted. She really wasn't frightened of very much, and she could be quite ruthless with herself when it was necessary. In the end she gave up drink and cigarettes, two of her great pleasures, and I said, 'Ma'am I do admire your strength.'

'Nothing to admire, Anne,' she said. 'I knew I had to do it.'

That was her way, and her attitude of no-nonsense bravery was something I admired and tried to emulate. She went through some terrible times and faced up to them with great resolution and not a shred of self-pity. She hated the idea of divorce, and resisted for a long time but I watched as Tony Snowdon placed her in an impossible position, demeaning her and goading her into making it inevitable. I was terribly impressed by how she coped with the pain and distress of such a public falling-apart, but I was sorry she had to go through it. Seeing how she kept going was an inspiration to me when I had to deal with the aftermath of Christopher's accident and the deaths of Henry and then Charlie.

Our relationship was built on mutual respect and friendship. Princess Margaret also trusted me, which was an enormous compliment and helped me to deal confidently with the myriad issues that life with her could give rise to. So often life with Colin could feel oppressive, dealing with one problem after another, so my only role seemed to be to clear up after him. With Princess Margaret I could feel useful, be trusted by her to do a good job, and also have great companionship and fun.

It all stood me in good stead. I find, these days, that my family often ring me up for advice or to ask me to intercede gently with someone else and sort out a difficult situation. I find it rather wonderful that they want to turn to someone as old as me, but obviously my diplomatic training is now an asset for life.

CHAPTER SEVEN

Adventurer

ONE OF THE reasons I married Colin was the sense of adventure he seemed to embody. I knew I wanted a family, but I also wanted some glamour and excitement in my life, and the chance to travel. My marriage certainly provided all of that. Marrying Colin was a giant leap into the unknown, but I will never regret the many adventures we had and everything they've taught me.

I have discovered that taking risks encapsulates a certain attitude to life – a kind of open-mindedness and a desire for fresh experiences. It's an attitude that doesn't just enrich your own life, but can help you to understand the lives of others and the extraordinary variety and beauty in the world. Living life is about risks, big and small, and challenging yourself to do something even if you think there's a small chance it may end badly, or that you're a bit afraid of, is an excellent way to learn what you are capable of. I've sometimes been amazed by what I've been able to do when I take a deep breath and decide just to do it, risky or not. One can't learn anything new without taking a few chances.

My joy in being an adventurer began young. Holkham was a marvellous place to be a curious child, and my mother taught me to be bold, from climbing trees to sailing, and never to let fears of what might happen get in the way of a new experience. I have benefited a good deal from it. I also knew how to put up with a certain amount of physical discomfort, and if you're willing to do that, the opportunities for new experiences in life increase enormously.

I didn't know when I married Colin that the Glenconner motto is *Deus dabit vela* – God will fill the sails. It was peculiarly fitting as our marriage took us all over the world. In fact marriage to Colin meant almost constant travelling, even when we had young children. He introduced me to lots of new things, not least life in the West Indies, where I learned so much about an existence, climate and attitude totally different from the ones I'd been born to. He took an enormous risk in buying Mustique, and for a while it seemed that Tony Armstrong-Jones's name for the island 'Mustake', was appropriate, but I'm very glad now that Colin did buy it. Even during those early years the contrast between Mustique and London was so extreme it always struck me as funny, and our Spartan existence on the island had the benefit of heightening my appreciation of our glamorous London life.

Though I could never teach Colin the pleasures of being still from time to time, his appetite for seeing new places and meeting new people lent enormous richness to my life and the lives of our children.

Oddly, though, he didn't always enjoy the journeys. Colin was a nervous flier, which could make things difficult considering how much of it we did. I had a terrifying lesson quite early on in our marriage when we were on a plane going from Tahiti to New York. The pilot thought he would give us all a treat by soaring down so that we could take photographs of the islands.

As we went into a steep descent, Colin freaked. The door to the cockpit wasn't locked in those days, so he rushed straight into it and began to shout frantically at the pilot to take us up again. A pair of stewards had to manhandle him back to his seat and order me to calm him down. The whole plane was transfixed by the drama and it was so humiliating I started to cry. I didn't know then that I was going to have to learn to live with that kind of behaviour and develop a much thicker skin. In fact, it was early enough in our life together for him later to write me an apologetic note. After that the apologies stopped, but not, of course, the behaviour.

It did teach me that the only way to cope with Colin while travelling was to remain as calm as possible myself.

Getting worked up when one encounters difficulties never helps, while being friendly and reasonable can often smooth things over – and that's helped me in many situations since.

I had the chance to go on some extraordinary trips because of Colin's particular gift for friendship and because of the huge variety of people we met on Mustique. During one stay on the island in the early eighties, Sheikh Yamani, minister for oil in the Saudi Arabian government, arrived unexpectedly on the *Nabila*, a private yacht he had chartered. We watched the arrival of the enormous boat with interest and wondered if whoever was on board would want to come ashore. A message was sent over and we received a reply to the effect that Sheikh Yamani did not want to disembark and that the yacht would just be mooring for a while and move on. So Colin said, 'Okay, fine with us.'

What we didn't realise was that the sheikh expected to be implored with letters and messages to change his mind. Our failure to do so obviously bemused him and even, dare I say it, left him a little put out. Shortly afterwards another message arrived. The sheikh had now decided that, if Lord Glenconner was available, he might like a little trip around the island.

Colin said he'd be delighted, and not long afterwards, the sheikh and his entourage of burly security men came ashore. We quickly became friends and were invited on to the *Nabila*, which was an extraordinary floating palace, with a cinema, helipads, endless luxurious suites and a saloon hung with Picassos. It was so special, it actually became a movie star, appearing in the James Bond film *Never Say Never Again*. We all got on very well and waved goodbye, the best of friends.

Later he stayed with us at Glen, and invited us to visit him in Riyadh, which sounded like a wonderful opportunity to explore a new country. We arrived during Ramadan to stay in the hills in his summer retreat, which was, by Saudi Arabian standards, a fairly simple residence, though still very luxurious.

The sheikh invited us to dine in the desert one evening and it was an unforgettable experience. We went out to where black Bedouin tents had been erected between the sand dunes. It was a magical sight, and as we arrived, a splendid feast was being prepared for us. We were seated on cushions, surrounded by the light of lanterns with the stars glittering above, when we heard a thundering noise. We looked up and out of the darkness we suddenly saw a huge phalanx of horsemen riding straight at us at great speed. They seemed not to slow down at all as they approached and were only inches away when they stopped dead in front of us. The horses' noses were practically touching ours. It was a remarkable feat of horsemanship, and an incredible thing to witness, but it took every bit of the courage my mother had taught me not to flinch in that last moment.

Then it was time to eat. A sheep had been freshly killed and, sitting on a carpet, we watched as they began to serve.

Before it was my turn, the sheikh said to me: 'We are so pleased you are here and have something special for you as our honoured guest.'

I did my best to disguise my horror as he then presented me with a sheep's eye on a silver platter. I'm afraid that was one new thing I wasn't willing to try. Sheep's eyes apparently symbolise wifely devotion to her husband, but whatever the symbolism, I couldn't think of much that was less appealing. There was no way I could hide it under the vegetables as I'd learned to do from Princess Margaret, but of course neither did I want to offend our hosts. I'd spent enough time as lady in waiting by this point to have gained some experience in negotiating sticky diplomatic situations and thinking on my feet.

'How kind,' I said, 'but is there any other bit of the sheep that would also count as such an honour?'

'Yes, indeed,' said the sheikh, quite happily, and a piece of the liver was produced instead. What a relief. It was infinitely preferable to the eye. Apart from that, the feast was absolutely delicious.

It was a challenging experience in other ways too. We were learning a different culture and customs and found there was no easy way to take our leave. Every time we said we must be going, we were pressured to stay another night, and it was impossible to say no. Eventually we took advice from another Englishman, Patrick Beresford, who was there advising the sheikh on security.

Patrick explained that our mistake was to give advance warning. 'What you need to do is pack your suitcases, put on your hats and gloves, and just wait in the hall.'

It proved to be the right advice. We were finally able to take our leave, and head for our flight. We hadn't had a drop of alcohol since our arrival, so we both fell on the tray of drinks the stewards had waiting for us. But that trip is one of my happiest memories of travelling with Colin. We laughed a lot together and it reminded me that, whatever else was going on in our marriage and in our lives, there were still times when we could be good friends and just enjoy each other's company.

Having the right travelling companion can make all the difference when setting off on a journey. It is very important to find someone you can travel easily with, both metaphorically and practically. Even if you have great friends whom you love, travelling can bring out the worst in anyone and it can be very irritating to be with someone who is constantly complaining or making a fuss. I found to my great pleasure that my friend Margaret Vyner and I travelled extremely well together. We were always polite and considerate towards each other, which is vital, and we were also interested in the same things, which is just as important. It would be awful to find oneself somewhere full of interesting shops and galleries to visit and find one's companion wanted to stay by the hotel pool. You also need to be able to find a comfortable rhythm together. Some people like to have every day packed with activity, while others prefer to leave their itineraries to chance. I like a mix. It's useful to have some fixed points in a trip, and some ideas about what one wants to do, but I like to leave some room to be able to improvise, as well as a chance to sit back and soak in the atmosphere of wherever I am in an unhurried fashion. A shared sense of humour is also essential: you need to be able to laugh at the ridiculous moments that happen on any trip, and know how to tease each other back into a good humour. The small things matter too. Margaret and I both enjoyed playing cards, which can pleasantly wile away time on journeys, and has other advantages as we soon discovered!

We once visited the hill stations of Sri Lanka, where one could find old-fashioned clubs to stay in. In the evenings, red-faced elderly chaps would come in to prop up the bars and drink their gin and tonic, and occasionally they would offer to play bridge with us. Margaret and I would accept, acting innocently and not giving any impression that we were actually rather good. I've always loved playing cards, and bridge in particular was often played for hours when we were having country-house weekends. Both Margaret and I were experienced players. After a while, they would say rather accusingly, 'Oh, I say, you're not beginners at all, are you?' Of course, we hadn't said we were: they'd just assumed that, as women, we wouldn't be any good. It was very satisfying when we won. I remember one fellow looking most put out and saying, 'I didn't expect card sharps to look like you two!'

Margaret and I travelled together every year for twenty-six years, very often to India, which I'd loved right from my first visit back in the eighties. I adored the endless colour and excitement, and for some reason I felt completely at home there from the moment I stepped off the plane. I told Margaret we absolutely must go back together and she was as enthusiastic as I was. We loved scouring the wonderful little shops in Delhi and Jaipur, where there are so many beautiful objects, clothes and jewellery. Margaret was very artistic and had a marvellous eye, so we would go and explore India's rich artistic heritage together.

We were taught how to travel in India by Mitchell Crites, an American who had gone to live in India in 1960 and who dealt in art, antiques and objects. Having a friend who really knows the country you are exploring is worth its weight in gold, especially when it's someone like Mitch, who was so knowledgeable about the things we loved. He was incredible to us, and so kind. He took us to visit artists and craftsmen in tiny villages, so we actually got to see these beautiful paintings, textiles and sculptures being made. I still have several pieces in my house in Norfolk, which I bought in those villages and each one is a reminder of a very special time in that wonderful country.

Margaret and I recently had lunch with Mitch in London and when he saw us he put out his hands and said, 'Ah!

My girls!' I thought that was very funny as I was about to celebrate my ninetieth birthday, and Margaret is much the same age. When I laughed, Mitch simply shook his head and said, 'You'll always be my girls,' which was very touching.

Of course, if you're really going to have an adventure, sometimes you want to leave your guide behind and take the risk to launch yourself off into the unknown. From Mitch, we got our confidence, learned a little about how the country worked and how to behave, and soon Margaret and I were able to travel independently in India, which we loved. We went off the beaten track, where other tourists never went, setting off in taxis and heading wherever we wanted, though we did take the precaution of taking a cricket bat, along with a mandatory bottle of medicinal vodka. The vodka proved very welcome. We could always find tinned tomato juice and lemons, so would have a Bloody Mary in the evening wherever we ended up as we discussed the events of the day, but we never needed the cricket bat. We felt perfectly safe, despite being women travelling alone, partly because we found India to be a very welcoming country, and also because we didn't fuss or create problems.

Travelling with Margaret was always a joy. Perhaps because my husband was a difficult man, we were practised in the art of getting by without complaint and in a friendly manner. We also made each other laugh. Some ladies might have been enraged or frightened to find themselves staying overnight in a brothel and having to use a field as a lavatory, but we opened the bottle of vodka and had a very amusing evening listening to all the comings and goings. We simply treated it as another adventure. The next night our hotel was particularly luxurious, and I think we enjoyed it even more because of the contrast.

One of the best sails I ever had was also in India during one of my trips with Margaret. We were on the edge of the Coromandel Sea and I was desperate to find out what sailing there would be like. It wasn't anything we had planned or on any usual tourist itinerary. We simply decided to go down to the shore and see if there was a suitable boat for hire. We spotted a boat I was sure I'd be able to manage and negotiated hiring it for a few hours. It was a traditional wooden boat of the region, with a single sail and a huge heavy rudder. The man in charge warned me, 'A lady can't go out on her own!' He really wanted to send someone with me.

As sailing can be dangerous, one should always listen to the locals, but I've also learned that men, the world over, tend to underestimate women and their skills, and sitting there doing nothing while someone else did the sailing was not what I had my heart set on. I realised the owner was only concerned because he thought I wouldn't be able to handle the boat, not because there were difficult tides or winds, so I insisted on going alone. Margaret reassured them that I knew what I was doing, which helped, though she was less of a sailor herself and decided to stay on shore.

She later told me that as I sailed away the onlookers had stood looking after me, speechless with surprise. As I disappeared out of sight around the headland, there had been quite a commotion, everyone frantic they might never see me again. Fortunately I was oblivious, enjoying a magnificent sail – so beautiful, so romantic and so warm. I didn't know a sea like that existed. If I had fallen in, it would have been a lovely warm bath. It was one of the most magical, unforgettable moments of my life. I arrived back ashore in a reasonably creditable manner, much to their relief and amazement.

In Mustique the waters and bays are heavenly for swimming, but there I know it's definitely not safe to sail without someone who knows the area intimately. The tides are very strong and the winds can be tricky. Being adventurous and pushing oneself to explore is wonderful, but I would always caution against being reckless.

Unfortunately, I learned it was positively dangerous to explore India with Colin as he very often created scenes and people there were less inclined to be as forgiving of his antics as they were in the West Indies. Mitch again was on hand to guide us, but more than once we had to make a hasty getaway when Colin's behaviour was turning the atmosphere into something unpleasant and Mitch sensed real danger.

Mitch did a great deal of business with Colin, from whom he says he learned just as much as he taught, but while

Margaret and I loved taking our time making our decisions about what to buy, Colin's compulsive need to acquire things could send him into a frenzy. Colin loved nothing so much as shops, but was always in such a desperate rush to get to the next one that it was hard to enjoy the one we were in. We went on one trip to India when he was building his house in St Lucia and was obsessed with buying things for it. He would make taxis scream to a halt when something caught his eye that he just had to have – even when things were clearly not for sale. Once, we were driving down a street with Mitch, and Colin saw the door of a house he absolutely had to have.

'I'll take a photograph of it, and get it made up for you,' Mitch said.

'No!' Colin declared. 'I want *that* one.'

So Mitch, who could speak fluent Hindi, negotiated an irresistible offer with the owner, who then unhinged his door and watched it being carried away. The same thing happened further down the street, where Colin bought someone's windows. The old lady who owned the house wasn't there, but her son sold them anyway. I tried not to think about her amazement when she would return home to discover she no longer had any windows. I hope Mitch gave them a very good deal. The one time shopping in India with Colin was a pleasure was when we were staying in a gorgeous floating palace for a few days in Kashmir. Every morning the local traders would come alongside in their canoes with all sorts of fabrics, clothes and local crafts and Colin could select what he wanted while lounging on the deck. He was much more relaxed when the shops came to him.

Colin at his best could be an inspiring travel companion. He could talk so knowledgeably about art and architecture that he could bring a city to life. Nowadays I rely on knowledgeable friends, and reading as much as I can about a place before I visit. I also like reading about it after I get back, and I have quite a library of books about India and Indian art now tucked away in Norfolk.

I have become a very good packer for warm climates when I travel. I always put in a few long cotton dresses for dinner, and for my most recent trip, I bought a new swimming costume with sleeves, which is very reassuring for the older figure. Colin always travelled with a straw basket containing a bottle of vodka, a snorkel and a mask in case the plane he was travelling in ditched in the sea, and a pashmina he used to sleep under. When I get on an aeroplane, these days, my priorities are comfortable clothes and a good book. For many years while travelling, I wore cotton *kurta* tops and trousers, softly flowing, comfortable and easy to move in – the ones that inspired Colin to wear the same for the rest of his life. They are absolutely marvellous in hot climates.

I have taken a certain amount of care over the years to look after myself in the sun. For one thing, I've always loved hats. I've worn them ever since I was a child, when we were made to wear straw hats when we went to the beach. I think that might have had a lot to do with why my skin has survived all those months in the West Indies and my travels in hot places like India. We didn't understand as much about the damaging effects of UV rays on skin in the sixties and seventies, and didn't take care to wear sun creams, but I'm very glad I didn't go as far as some of my friends who would coat themselves in olive oil and lie in the sun, or even use silver foil to reflect the rays back onto their faces and get a deeper tan.

Nowadays, the travel associated with my book has been one of the most exciting aspects of my new career as an author. I was getting rather used to just being down in Norfolk, and had forgotten how energising and exciting it is to see new places and meet fascinating new people. It has renewed my resolve to continue to travel as far afield as I can for as long as I am able. I would love to go to New Zealand. I think it would be a marvellous place to visit and, thanks to my New Zealand grandmother, I have family there it would be a delight to get to know. I have to take things a little slower now, as I do tire more quickly than I used to, but I still hope to get there, as well as to return to the United States, where I have so many friends and so many happy memories.

I still get out to Mustique to stay with a dear friend and I also have a wonderful friend who takes me for summer trips on his yacht. I've been lucky enough to go several times now and have always loved to swim from the boat. This year I let him know I was worried I wouldn't be able to manage the ladder into the sea any more. He said he had taken care of that and had arranged for a hoist to get me into and out of the water. I said, 'That's wonderful but how on earth do I get into and out of the hoist?'

'Someone will go with you and help you.'

It sounded very funny, not just for me but for anyone watching, and I was up for the attempt. It would be worth any amount of being pushed into hoists and lifted about if it meant I could enjoy the bliss of swimming in the sea.

The 'hoist' turned out to be a very useful swimming platform, so between that and the swimming costume, I could really be free to enjoy myself. I firmly believe in keeping moving and I am still a strong swimmer. I always recommend it as a form of exercise that is both relaxing and invigorating at the same time.

Shortly after my eightieth birthday, I had an opportunity to travel to Ethiopia – a country that had always been on my 'bucket list' as I wanted to see some of the medieval rock churches in a mountainous region in the heart of the country. Unbeknownst to me, some could only be reached through very narrow tunnels. We had to go in on our hands and knees and I had a lady in front of me – her bottom in my face – who halfway through the tunnel, suffered a panic attack and froze. It took some while but eventually I managed to calm her down so that we were able to move on again but it seemed as if we were stuck in that narrow tunnel for ages.

Towards the end of the trip, we were due to head off up a mountain to see some rare rabbit but by now I was suffering from terrible altitude sickness and, along with two friends, decided to return to Addis Ababa early before flying home. Though memorable, the trip had turned out to be like a teenage backpacking holiday. On my return to the UK, looking somewhat exhausted, my children pointed out that I really was far too old to be crawling on my hands and knees through tunnels.

My risk-taking might be a bit more limited now, but I will always respond with excitement to the magical words I heard first from my governess, Billy Williams, so many years ago: 'Let's go and explore.' I'm still blessed with energy and never give up the chance to discover something new. It doesn't have to be far afield. One thing the restrictions around Covid have taught many of us is that there are wonderful places to explore on our doorstep. I adore the landscape of Norfolk. Even after living here so long I still find new corners I haven't visited before, and familiar places are full of surprise and interest. I'm so glad I live near the sea. It has brought me fun and excitement and joy (and a few hairy moments) but it has also brought me peace at moments of crisis. When I am in London, I spend my time in different ways, seeing as many of my friends and family as I can, going to theatres and exhibitions, and taking every opportunity to go to concerts. Much as I love my Alexa, there is nothing to replace seeing a live performance.

Doing something different, taking a risk, embracing a new experience, or just turning down an unfamiliar street, I firmly believe that we are never too old to have an adventure.

CHAPTER EIGHT

Friend

MY CLOSEST FRIENDS have been a bedrock of support to me and I don't think I could have managed any of the roles I've played in my life without them. I have been blessed with some lifelong friendships, some from school, some through family, others through my marriage. Of course, the longer one lives, the more friends go ahead of one and I miss them terribly. The memory of them, though, is still a source of comfort and pleasure.

When I was young I gained courage and fresh perspective from friends, and as I grew older I found that my close female friends in particular were a vital support. They have been great providers of joy, advice and reassurance, and I couldn't have managed being a wife, mother, lady in waiting or author without them. I do believe that, chosen wisely, our closest friends bring out the best in us, remind us of what our own strengths are, and encourage us in the right ways. That is what my friends have done for me over the years, and I very much hope I have done the same for them.

Of course, life often chooses our friends for us. My sister Carey and I used to love playing with the children in the village, but when we moved into Holkham Hall, having the physical barrier of the park walls as well as a long driveway, we weren't able to keep up those friendships, so we came to rely more on each other.

Carey and I were always both sisters and friends. We understood each other in the particular way siblings do, and enjoyed sharing activities, riding our bikes or ponies, round Holkham when we were little and going to dances at the local airbase when we got a bit older, sneaking into the house through the coal chute when we came back late. Those times formed bonds that stood the test of time. Naturally we had our moments and one of those was when I was chosen to be maid of honour at the Coronation. It was hard on Carey to be left out of a once-in-a-lifetime occasion, with all the fuss and attention it brought with it. Our friendship survived it, though, and we remained very fond of each other all our lives, and loved watching each other's children grow up. Though Carey never took to sailing, her son James did and I'm delighted he now helps run the boathouse at Burnham Overy Staithe, as my mother and I did in the past. My mother was a keen sailor and, with a group of friends, bought the boathouse just after the war to ensure it was never redeveloped and this vital asset to the sailing community remained in perpetuity.

Carey and I also saw a lot of our Ogilvy cousins, who became our friends too, learning to reel with them at Downie Park during the war, then seeing each other for holidays and parties in the years that followed. They were the only men I knew when I came out, which made them so valuable as friendly faces in a ballroom full of strangers. I also have a much younger sister, Sarah, and because of the age gap I'm afraid we treated her rather more as a doll! Sadly, Carey died a few years ago so having Sarah is very precious. Carey's sons are a similar age to my children so now there is another generation of cousins who have shared holidays and memories, just as I did with mine.

Having relied on my family friendships for years, it took me a while to make other friends at school. I was shy, so instinctively drawn to girls who could make me feel relaxed and laugh as well as excite my curiosity. Caroline Blackwood, who later married Lucien Freud and then the poet Robert Lowell, always fascinated me. She was clever, but dreamy at the same time with a unique way of looking at the world. I thought she was marvellous, and once we'd left school and embarked on new lives, I admired her talent as a writer. Strong as our friendship was at school and for some time after, it sadly didn't stand the test of time. Our lives moved in different directions. She went to live in America for quite a long period, and we drifted apart. But I still have such vivid and fond memories of how she befriended me as a rather lost schoolgirl.

Sarah Henderson, who I also met at school, has been one of the great constants in my life. Sarah and I still see each other often. Although she lives some distance away, near Stratford-upon-Avon, we talk on the telephone two or three times a week, and have a tradition of seeing Shakespeare plays together. She is still the person I turn to, other than my children, when I want to talk through practical problems, unpick some knotty conundrum or talk about other things that time and weeding alone can't solve. Sarah was a frequent visitor at Glen, always giving me lots of practical help from arranging the flowers to taking the children shooting and fishing. I have so many happy memories of being with her there, setting the world to rights in my sitting room. Sarah's speciality was knitting shooting stockings. Her fingers would flash away, and she wouldn't even have to look. Women friends who came to stay would often be occupied with tatting or smocking or something while we chatted together in those days. A favourite of mine was tapestry.

Sarah and Princess Margaret made quite a formidable team. They were both staying at Glen when my father died, and took over the running of the house while I went down to Norfolk to help my mother. Colin was a bit put out that I had left them in charge as he thought they were trying to take him in hand, but he appreciated and respected them both, so just grumbled to me long distance while they made sure everything at Glen went on as smoothly as ever. Old friendships like mine and Sarah's, where you have seen each other through the strange vicissitudes of life, are especially valuable. We can allow ourselves to be sad as we remember those we have lost, but also relive all the wonderful and funny times we have spent together over the years.

I was still very shy when I came out so making friends was difficult. I'm glad I had my schoolfriends and cousins, but I still felt like a bit of a wallflower during those early years. I try to remember that now, as I've discovered it's so often the case that people who seem to be holding themselves aloof and looking a bit superior, are often just shy. I try to make a special effort with them now, as I remember what it was like to feel rather awkward at parties.

When I married Colin, I discovered he shared my fondness for family connections and in fact several of the women who became my closest friends were relations of his. That network of cousins was the foundation of our social world, despite the many other people we met. I told him more than once I would have married him for his cousins. In fact, our parties on Mustique were often family affairs with most of the guests being brothers, sisters, cousins and their families. Having a rock star like Mick Jagger there, or Princess Margaret, gave them a reputation for being glamorous, which Colin's salesman side encouraged, but welcome as they were, they were only a small part of the guest list.

Our summers at Glen were largely extended family times. So many friendships were formed and deepened while we were there. The men would go out and shoot, and I, with the wives who were interested, would join them for lunch in one of the bothies, the traditional small stone cottages dotted around the estate. It was beautiful with the heather in bloom no matter what the weather was like, though in my memory it was always sunny. After lunch we'd often play with the children in the swimming-pool, and when the men came back from shooting they'd join us until it was time to dress for dinner. We'd put Floris bath oils in all of the bathrooms, so the whole house would smell lovely as everyone got ready. Then we'd congregate for drinks and dinner, and afterwards, if Colin wasn't in the midst of amateur dramatics, there would be singsongs or card games until we headed off for bed.

The pattern of the days meant the women got the chance to spend lots of time together, and much as I have loved the men in my life, and been fond of many male friends, it was the women I found I could most rely on for easy companionship and laughter. The author Susanna 'Zanna' Johnston was a cousin of Colin's on his mother's side and had some of the Paget eccentricity and impulsivity. I wrote and edited *The Picnic Papers* with her, and she was one of the best storytellers I ever knew on or off the page. I laughed more with her than with anyone else, and I always admired the confidence with which she got on with life, never minding the judgement of others. Her escapades always had me in fits of laughter, and while her husband, Nicky, was calm and scholarly, she was a whirlwind of energy. She was also a rather naughty mimic and, like me, enjoyed being teasing about anyone she thought was pompous or dull. The world was brighter when she was around, and her novels were just like her, full of fun and wit, creativity and a devil-may-care wildness. I was such an admirer of her writing, I felt a little shy sending her *Lady in Waiting* when it was published, having only just begun writing in my eighties, but she was so generous about it and wholeheartedly celebrated the success of the book. Being with Zanna, or just talking to her on the phone, always lifted my spirits and meant I felt more able to cope with life. She was like Colin in that way, always fizzing with ideas and stories, without so many of his rages.

Margaret Vyner, my favourite travelling companion, I met through Colin. She was another huge support to me during married life. We shared so much in common that we often both knew exactly how we were feeling without having to explain. Margaret offered vodka and sympathy, and talking to her always helped me gain a fresh perspective. She helped me be less upset about Colin, reminding me that what he did wasn't my fault. She always knew how to distract me from my troubles. Her husband, Henry, had a terrible gambling problem and lost his estate at the card table. She never complained, but got on with the business of raising their children and adapting as the family's circumstances changed. As a result she understood the financial ups and downs in our own family as Colin sold houses or pictures with hardly any warning, spent a fortune on something one minute, then declared we had to economise ruthlessly the next. Friends who know you so well, who have been through similar experiences and can make you feel better, are a tremendous comfort.

Colin's spending was often outrageous, but he was never a gambler. Henry gambled at the Claremont, John Aspinall's club, which was situated above Annabel's in Mayfair. Lord Lucan, who famously and suspiciously disappeared after his nanny was murdered, was part of the same small set. The mystery still intrigues people today, as it was clearly his wife who was intended as the murder victim rather than the nanny, but if Henry ever knew what happened to Lucan, he never told Margaret. She and I thought Lucan must have killed himself and that his friend Aspinall had fed his body to the tigers at his private zoo in Kent. We had no idea why he'd want to conceal his own death, but we could certainly see it would work as vengeance, making his wife suffer through years of uncertainty. That group of men were incredibly close, and even though Henry and Lucan lost millions at Aspinall's, they were all absolutely loyal to each other and never let the secret slip. It's rather impressive. None of my friendships have ever involved dark secrets like that, thank goodness.

The very best friendships survive rough patches, deepen with time and become a source of enormous strength as well as fun. They also work to support each other.

Ingrid Channon was another cousin of Colin's who became one of my closest friends. Ingrid was a great support for me when Charlie was in the throes of his addiction and while Christopher was so ill. She was married to Paul Channon, son of Henry 'Chips' Channon, the politician, author and diarist, who renovated their marvellous house, Kelvedon Hall, in Essex. It is a glorious red-brick Georgian country house, and Ingrid would often invite the children and me to stay there. You'd never know you were only forty-five minutes from London. Kelvedon had a lovely garden, a donkey, horses and a bluebell wood where we all had picnics. There was also a heated pool, which looked like a Roman bath. It was surrounded with stone, and thrilled the children. It was a refuge for me during the early years of marriage to Colin, and I'm sure she knew that.

Everything changed for Ingrid after the tragic death of her eldest daughter. Olivia died of an overdose just after finishing her finals at Oxford in 1986. Ingrid was naturally devastated, and angry with the other young people who'd been at the party before Olivia died. It was a dreadful time for both of us. I was dealing with Charlie going in and out of rehab, and dreaded every day getting the news that he had overdosed. Olivia was vibrant, full of wit and seemed to have a wonderful life ahead of her. Her death came out of the blue and was a terrible shock. Drugs took an awful toll on Ingrid and me as we were so naive about them.

Christopher's accident came only about a year after Olivia's death, but that didn't stop Ingrid being a tower of strength for me, which shows just what a remarkable woman she was. She visited him all the time, and would often drive him to his physiotherapy appointments to give me a rest once he was out of hospital. I really don't think I could have managed without her. It was so generous of her that, even though she was heartbroken and still deeply angry about Olivia's death, she made every effort to support me, emotionally and practically, as I tried to save my own child. I am so sorry, though, that Ingrid could never forgive and was still angry. I tried to tell her how forgiveness had been essential to me in the aftermath of Christopher's accident, then when Henry and Charlie died. It allowed me to go on and celebrate their lives, and I found it gave me the strength to look after Christopher as he slowly recovered and adjusted.

'It was different for me,' she would say. 'I couldn't say goodbye to Olivia.'

Ingrid was never able to go to Olivia's grave. I would visit and take flowers and she'd ask me to put flowers there for her too. I'd ask her to come with me, but she couldn't face it. Taking her flowers seemed a small thing to do, but at least it was something.

'You're so lucky,' she said. 'You've got a faith, and I haven't.'

'You don't need to have faith,' I'd reply, 'but you do need to forgive, because until you can get that poison out of your system, you won't be able to breathe properly.'

But Ingrid couldn't do it. I wondered if by hanging on to the anger, she felt she was also hanging on to Olivia in some way. We accommodated our differences, and beyond a certain point, I couldn't push things but just had to respect her feelings and offer what comfort I could.

I watched another good friendship flounder in the aftermath, and the break-up of two close friends is very painful to see. One of the young people at the fatal party was Zanna's daughter. In the trial that followed, she was convicted of supplying the fatal dose, though she wasn't a dealer and had just picked up the drugs at Olivia's request. Zanna wanted Ingrid and Paul to appeal for leniency, which in their shock and heartbreak they simply couldn't do. It was all terrible. The press love writing about heirs and heiresses, titles, drugs and curses, as they did around the deaths later of both Charlie and Henry, but for us at the centre of it, it was nothing short of horrific. They never seemed to realise they were talking about actual living people, who were prey to the same temptations and pressures as everyone else.

Ingrid and Zanna never spoke again, but they were both at Christopher's wedding when he married his first wife Anastasia. When I saw across the church that it looked like they might end up seated next to each other, I asked

Sarah Henderson to sit between them, which she did, in the most tactful manner, saving them all a difficult encounter. Of course, there was no scene. Both Ingrid and Zanna had thrown everything into helping me and Christopher when they were still in the midst of their troubles, and both shared in my delight at seeing him married, but I was so sorry that their own friendship ended. Just recently, at my ninetieth birthday party, it was poignant, and also lovely, to see their daughters chatting together, so I hope those family troubles will now heal for the generation that follows.

My heart broke for Ingrid. I wished I'd been able to convince her of the power of forgiveness, but it wasn't possible. I simply continued to love and support both Ingrid and Zanna and neither of them ever asked me to choose between them. I'm sure they would have done the same for me. Ingrid died in 2009, and Zanna in 2022 and I miss them both more than I can say.

Friends and husbands don't always go together, but Colin loved my close friends. He realised how much I needed them, and was always delighted to see them. He respected their intelligence and wit, their curiosity and kindness, and he loved to spoil them. They were always at the top of the guest list for the grand parties in Mustique, and in turn they appreciated the good in him rather than condemning him, laughing and marvelling over his excesses, which was just what I wanted and needed.

I never told any of my friends about what happened to me on Mustique. They saw some of Colin's behaviour, so I wouldn't be surprised if they put two and two together, but we never spoke about the violence. It was my decision to tell only my mother about that day. Even in the closest of friendships, one has to respect what we choose to keep private. In truth, I don't think I would have known how to approach talking about it even with my closest friends when I was having such difficulty myself in coming to terms with it.

Instead we made Colin's behaviour into a joke. They would say, 'Anne, what is the matter with your husband?' when he had done something terrible. Being able to laugh at his excesses with them made it bearable, though through all the years we discussed him, we never did come up with an answer that satisfied us. Instead I drew enormous strength from shared laughter and their many practical kindnesses.

Colin and I were lucky to have so many shared friendships. It certainly doesn't happen in every marriage I've observed. I was very fond of many of Colin's friends and admired his ability to discover and nurture so many new ones. He was a good friend of Princess Margaret's long before we became close again, and without him I would never have got to know Rupert and Josephine Loewenstein so well. It is Josephine I visit now when I go to Mustique. Mostly Colin's friends saw only a little of his bad side, and a lot of what was best in him, which was always his infectious exuberance, so they made excuses or ignored the worst and concentrated on the positive, much as I did myself. I do feel glad that Colin and I managed to maintain a real friendship during our marriage. When he was happy, he really was the most marvellous companion.

I'm afraid I didn't like all his friends, though. At one stage he spent a lot of time with Michael Winner, the film director and restaurant critic, and they struck up quite a rapport. For once, Colin seemed to have met his match when it came to bad behaviour, and he was wide-eyed and thrilled at what Michael did. Michael was an epic complainer in restaurants with absolutely no shame. He liked nothing better than to tear strips off people, insult the food and make the most almighty fuss. He didn't mind people staring – in fact, he loved it. Of course, he and Colin adored behaving appallingly together, egging each other on like two naughty schoolboys. In fact, I can safely say that the only person who liked going out to eat with Colin was Michael Winner.

'If you think I'm bad,' Colin would say to me, 'Michael is much worse. Last time, we threw all our food on the floor!'

'That sounds awful.'

'No, I completely understand him,' Colin said. 'You must come out with us. It's great fun.'

That was obviously the last thing I wanted to do, and by that time I was confident enough to refuse to go anywhere with them.

For friendships to be at their best, they need to be kept up, preferably with decent periods of time spent together. I sometimes think that the ease of communication these days, with emails and text messages and social media, has actually made taking care of one's friendships more difficult. When we all had to make an effort to ring each other up and arrange a visit, we treasured our time together and made the most of it. Now it can feel as if everyone you know is available all the time, which perversely means one doesn't put in so much effort. I also find people checking their phones at meals or while I'm talking to them very off-putting. How strange to take the time to be with someone, then spend it checking for messages from people who aren't there at all! I would much rather enjoy the world around me with my own eyes than see everything through that funny little screen. You see it everywhere, people sitting together and not talking, each one staring at their phone, each in their own little bubble. I shall resist having one of the infernal things as long as possible.

When I drive up to Glen now, I stop on the way at the Morritt Hotel just off the A66. I used to feel shy eating there on my own, but now I'm perfectly happy and, rather than read a book, I enjoy my supper and watch everyone else. I'm always astonished by the number of couples who come out to eat together and never seem to exchange a word between them, just looking at their phones instead. Very odd.

Each stage of life shifts the pieces on the board, relation-ships change, people move around and old friendships can take on new life. Patricia Rawlings, who I have known for a very long time, now lives close to me. We are able to spend more time together and I adore her company. I met Tim Leese in Norfolk, and within five minutes, I knew we were going to be tremendous friends. He's very clever, very musical and never lets me get away with anything. We had a lovely holiday once, driving around Europe, and I found, just like Margaret Vyner, he was practical and funny and a very easy companion, whether we were staying in some beautiful apartment filled with flowers, or in a cramped house next to an oddly smelly factory. I was best man at his wedding, which was a great honour. I had ordered a rather nice wedding cake for him and his husband to be served at the wedding breakfast, but there was a mix-up in the kitchen and they came to the table with a child's birthday cake in the shape of a ship with sparklers for funnels. It wasn't quite what any of us were expecting. It did taste very nice and the restaurant, rather shamefacedly, took it off the bill.

My new career has opened the door to making new friends. Sometimes if a book festival is at a stately home, I'm invited to stay and it's like old times, only instead of sitting down to dinner with relations and friends, I dine with my fellow authors. It means I'm meeting so many people from very different backgrounds and interests, but we all have writing in common. I now know why people like joining professional organisations as we get to discuss all sorts of nitty-gritty details about being a writer that other people might think terribly dull or not understand at all, but it's great fun and illuminating for us.

I would never have been able to perform any of the roles I have played in life, without being supported and sustained by my friendships. They affect us in so many ways during our lives, as great examples in how to behave, and sometimes how not to. Their reactions and opinions affect our own. They can broaden or narrow our horizons, provide support and practical help. Friends, new and old, teach us so much.

In the end to have your family as your friends can be the greatest blessing. They are stuck with you and you with them, so far better you all get on. I now count my beloved daughters, Amy and May, as two of my very best friends. We can get on one another's nerves, of course, but we would do anything for each other. Christopher and Johanna are also amazing. It was predicted that by this stage of his life, Christopher would be in a wheelchair. He isn't. More than that, he is so loving and cheerful. 'I wouldn't be here if it wasn't for you, Mum,' he says all the time. He showers me with affection. He's also terribly proud of his daughters, Bella and Demitra, both of whom have graduated with first-class degrees. Whenever I see him or the girls I think of Ingrid, Zanna,

Margaret and Sarah and all those who were there to help him recover from his accident. I feel so incredibly grateful to have had such wonderful friends.

AND FINALLY . . .

AT MY NINETIETH birthday party this summer I sat under the statue of the goddess Diana, the one that belonged to Cicero many centuries ago, in the Long Gallery at Holkham. She is an old friend, at least two thousand years old, and, like everything in the Gallery, she reminds me of my grandfather, and the time we spent talking together there about the treasures of Holkham, and him introducing me to great classical music on his huge old gramophone.

For the day, Johanna's daughter, Jessica, had made wreaths for all the statues in the gallery to wear, and I was in my new dress and lucky brooch, so we were all looking our best. Cicero's Diana might be a good deal older than I am, but we have both witnessed a lot of history, so I loved having her watching over my shoulder as I celebrated.

I've seen such an enormous amount of change. The role of the aristocracy has largely disappeared from British public life, with the exception of the Royal Family. Where it does continue, it is doing so rather more quietly. Stately homes are now open to the public, though many still have private rooms where families continue to live in a manner maybe not too unlike what I knew when I was young, and working in a way that benefits the whole community.

I hope that through *Lady in Waiting* and this book I've opened a window on how my generation lived and thought, and I know that what seems ordinary to one generation will seem exotic and strange to another. The process goes in both directions, of course, as I puzzle over modern technology and manners.

I'm thrilled to have witnessed some remarkable moments in history. Seventy years on from the Coronation, it was wonderful again to play a small role in the Queen's Platinum Jubilee celebrations, sharing my memories of the day and having them recorded for posterity. I was interviewed in Westminster Abbey with Rosemary Muir (nee Spencer-Churchill) who was the highest-ranking maid of honour at the Coronation and is still today an absolute force of nature. She makes my old-fashioned way of speaking sound positively demotic, and as I gushed about how it had been one of the best days of my life, Lady Rosemary was saying it was really awfully inconvenient because she'd had to put off her wedding, and race back to Blenheim afterwards as her parents were holding a very large party, which involved roasting four oxen.

I watched with admiration how the Queen handled the transformation of society during her long reign – as well as handling the triumphs and tragedies within her own family with such dignity and skill. She once said she put it down to being well trained and I think there's a great deal of truth in that. I am very proud to know King Charles and the Queen Consort, and now that their turn has come, I think they'll do a magnificent job, just as the Queen did for so many years. I have every confidence too in the Prince and Princess of Wales when the roles fall to them.

No rank, fortune or training, though, can ever really prepare you for what life throws at you, or protect you from it. We are all learning as we go. I hope I am able to show, by example at the very least, that joy is always waiting for us somewhere in life, even in our darkest moments and often in the most surprising of ways, and that embracing life in all its strangeness has so much good to offer.

Of course there were guests I would have dearly loved to have at my party. I missed Charlie, Henry and Carey, but they were there in spirit as I watched their children chatting together. I even missed Colin, though he would have insisted on being the centre of attention and I am loving my turn in the spotlight now. Naturally I missed the friends I have lost along the way, like Princess Margaret, Zanna and Ingrid, but I was able to talk about them to my sister Sarah, who knew them all so well, and we laughed again over some of the more ridiculous stories. I won't pretend, though, that I sat at the table thinking deep thoughts about my life while watching everyone enjoy themselves. I was enjoying myself far too much, reliving old memories and making new ones.

Wherever I go now, I'm always being asked my secrets for a healthy long life. I'm not sure there are such secrets, but for me the key is, I think, that I've learned to strike a balance between pleasing myself and pleasing others. I know when to push myself and when to go easy. I try to savour life's pleasures, big and small, and count my blessings. I get a lot of strength from my family, my faith and from the beauty of the world. I value peace and rest as much as chatter and excitement. I try to keep abreast of things rather than sinking into my own little world, and a positive mindset is always a great asset. One can't sum up the learnings of a lifetime without sounding a little like a greetings card. It's difficult. These things sound like clichés but they are both simple and true.

I have tried to teach my children to be considerate, kind and curious adults. I certainly think they are rather wonderful, but now the process is reversed, and I find they're teaching me much more than I'm teaching them. I give them advice on gardening, remind them of who is related to whom, act as the family phone book, and show them how to correctly address people when letter-writing, but my family do so much more for me, helping me navigate all the strange new things one encounters in modern life and feeding my curiosity. They have introduced me to the joys of buying clothes on the internet, listening to all my favourite music on Alexa, the wonder of audio books, and shown me how to do interviews from my dining room on Zoom!

My friends continue to offer me hospitality, laughter and news, as well as all sorts of practical advice and help from how to get in and out of a boat to appearing on television.

When I was young, the world certainly seemed simpler. Perhaps that's always how it looks to someone of my age, but I felt one knew what was expected of a wife and a mother, a hostess or a lady in waiting. But then, of course, playing all those parts turned out to be rather different and I also discovered there were others I could turn my hand to as well. The roles one plays in life never entirely disappear. I will always be a daughter of a high ancestral name, and being a widow is still being a wife in a way. I aim never to stop being a hostess or a friend, and will be an adventurer as long as there are new things to look at in the world. I won't stop being an author either: it's far too much fun. Being a mother is also a role for life, but there comes a time when you realise you've done all you can and your children are responsible for their own decisions. I am very glad Christopher, Amy and May have made such good ones, and terribly sorry that Charlie didn't before he met his lovely wife and had Cody. He made an excellent choice then, and his last years were his best and happiest. Henry also married a wonderful woman, but was right to be honest about his sexuality. I am reminded of his kindness whenever I meet his friends. Charlie and Henry would be so proud of their sons. Cody qualified as a lawyer and is now in the banking sector, and Euan is an accomplished electrical engineer.

No one ever knows what will come next in life, and I expect I shall have all sorts of surprises, good and bad, in the years still ahead. I have so much left to learn, but, surrounded by my friends and family, that idea fills me with hope and enthusiasm. In the meantime I shall treasure the memory of my 'bonfire' of a birthday cake and stand by the promise I made to my guests – as I gathered my breath for the mighty task of blowing out ninety candles – 'I look forward to seeing you all here again in ten years' time.'

ACKNOWLEDGEMENTS

I WOULD FIRSTLY like to thank Johanna and Amy for their help with the book. To my editor, Rowena Webb, for believing in me and encouraging me in my new career as an author, thank you.

Also thank you to the editorial team behind the book: Tom Perrin, Kirstie Crawford and Imogen Roberts. And to the wider team at Hodder, especially Eleni Lawrence, Helen Flood and Juliet Brightmore, and at Curtis Brown my agent Gordon Wise. At Hachette Books US, I would like to thank Mollie Weisenfeld and Lauren Rosenthal.

Finally, I'd like to thank Princess Dora Loewenstein for suggesting the title of this book.

PICTURE ACKNOWLEDGEMENTS

Chapter 1

The Graham Norton Show on BBC television with Olivia Colman, Helena Bonham Carter and our host, November 2019. Photo © PA Images/Alamy Photo Stock.

Chapter 2

With my mother and sister Carey, 1935.
Author's collection.

Chapter 3

With Colin, Mustique, 1967.
Photo © Lichfield Archive via Getty Images.

Chapter 4

With Bob Hope at a pro-am golf tournament for the charity Scope, c. 1980.
Author's collection.

Chapter 5
Charlie's christening, 1957.
Photo © Henry Bush/ANL/Shutterstock.

Chapter 6
With Princess Margaret, Mustique, c. 1969.
Author's collection.

Chapter 7
Blissful day sailing my boat.
Author's collection.

Chapter 8
With my friend Susanna (Zanna) Johnston in 1983, when
we published Picnic Papers.
Author's collection.

Final photo
Blowing out the candles on my 90th birthday cake, 2022.
Photo © Nick Walter.

RESOURCES

SafeLives
https://safelives.org.uk/
Company number: 05203237
Registered charity number: 1106864
Scottish Charity reference number SCO48291
info@safelives.org.uk

Refuge
https://refuge.org.uk/
Telephone helpline: 0808 2000 247
Company number: 1412276.
Registered charity number: 277424.

Victim Support
https://www.victimsupport.org.uk/
Telephone helpline: 08 08 16 89 111
Registered charity number: 298028

Women's Aid

https://www.womensaid.org.uk/

info@womensaid.org.uk

Company number 3171880

Registered charity number: 1054154

THE TIMES MEMOIR OF THE YEAR

Out Now

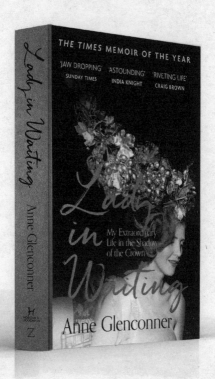

Discover the remarkable life of the Lady in Waiting to Princess Margaret who was also a Maid of Honour at the Queen's Coronation. Anne Glenconner reveals the real events behind *The Crown* as well as her own life of drama, tragedy and courage, with the wonderful wit and extraordinary resilience which define her.

A storm. A disappearance.
A race against time . . .

'Dazzling . . . full of glamour, intrigue and gossip'
TELEGRAPH MAGAZINE

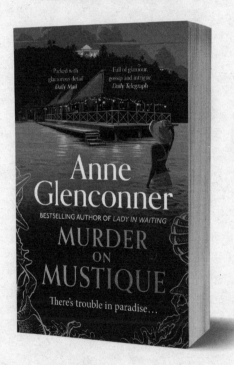

OUT NOW

Wartime secrets, intrigue and deceit abound at Holkham Hall in the thrilling new murder mystery from Anne Glenconner.

'[A] winning, well-plotted read.... the mystery's denouement at the dance makes a glamorous and dramatic conclusion'
DAILY MAIL

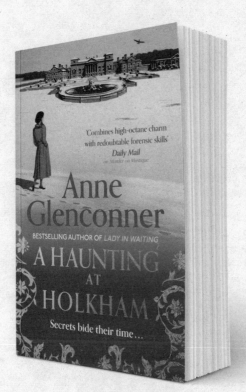

OUT NOW